GEOGRAPHICAL FACTORS IN INDIAN HISTORY

GEOGRAPHICAL FACTORS IN INDIAN HISTORY

BY

K. M. PANIKKAR

GYAN

Published by

Gyan Publishing House
5, Ansari Road
Daryaganj, New Delhi-110002
Phone: 011-47034999, 9811692060
E-mail: books@gyanbooks.com

Distribution Network
gyanbooks.com
India, USA, Canada, UK, Australia

ISBN: 978-81-212-5530-1 (HB)
First Published, 1955

2nd Impression 2024

Printed at: Gyan Press, Delhi.

GEOGRAPHICAL FACTORS IN INDIAN HISTORY
Author: K. M. PANIKKAR

GEOGRAPHICAL FACTORS IN INDIAN HISTORY

By K. M. PANIKKAR

GEOGRAPHICAL FACTORS IN INDIAN HISTORY

By

K. M. PANIKKAR

1955

BHARATIYA VIDYA BHAVAN

CHAUPATTY, BOMBAY

INTRODUCTION

I have attempted in the following pages a preliminary study of the effects of geography on the shaping of India's history. This is a subject which has so far received but little attention. Indeed it may be said that geography has been the most neglected subject of study in India. The lack of interest that the ancient Hindus showed in geography as a science persists even today.

Geography constitutes the permanent basis of every nation's history. It is not too much to say that it is one of the major factors that determine the historical evolution of a people. Indian historical thinking was necessarily confined to a large extent to the growth and decline of local dynasties with the result that the overall factors which shaped our life seldom entered into our calculations. But a nation can neglect geography only at its peril. Both the internal policies of a country and its external relations are governed largely by its unalterable geographical conditions and their relationships in space to other countries. To take one example: the maintenance of the unity of India now achieved for the first time, is our primary concern: but in order to do so successfully we should have a proper appreciation of the geographical obstacles which prevented such a consummation for so long a time. Again take the case of the sea. Though India is surrounded on three sides by the seas, and has been for over 450 years subjected to political and economic pressure by maritime powers, there is as yet no appreciation of the relation of sea power to Indian history. Another significant fact which may be noted here, as arising from our lack of understanding of geography in its relation to national life is that unlike China and Persia, India never had a foreign policy till the British established their authority over it. We were neither maritime nor continental in our outlook.

To day Free India has to realise her position in the world, where geography has placed her in relation to other countries. She has also to understand the strength and weaknesses arising from her geography. The present study claims to be nothing more than a preliminary attempt to draw attention to some of the major aspects of this vast problem.

Cochin, K. M. PANIKKAR.
January, 1955.

CONTENTS

ILLUSTRATIONS

CHAPTER I

GENERAL

Geopolitics or the relation of geography with political processes is, generally speaking a new subject in historical and political studies. For long, geography was considered only a study of the earth's surface in relation to its physical formations, of mountains and rivers, plains and deserts, of oceans and seas and bays—the distance, relationships, directions, etc., necessary for the normal life of the people. Later, it became clear that climates, winds, currents and other natural phenomena which affected human life were parts of geographical study. In the nineteenth century there came into existence a school, the most notable exponent of which was Buckle, which emphasised the connection between civilisation and geography. However, it is only in the twentieth century that world conceptions of geography began to affect political thinking in a fundamental manner.

The originator of this new way of thinking was Sir Halford Mackinder whose essay, the *Geographical Pivot of History,* may well be considered the beginning of geopolitical thought. With Mackinder's theory we shall deal later at some length. Here it is sufficient to emphasise that Mackinder thought of the Afro-Eurasian Continent as the world island and the new hemisphere as only a smaller island detached from the world island. He was the first to look upon the world as a single geographical entity and the thing that struck him as a geographer was the fact that what he called the heartland, the vast area of the interior which could not be touched by sea power, was continuously pressing on to the sea coasts. His grandiose theories, elaborated further in his *Democratic Ideals and Realities*, found unexpected support in German thinkers notably Haushofer and his school, who developed their doctrines from the special point of view of Germany and made them in a measure the basis of the military thinking of Hitler and his generals.

What Haushofer made of geopolitics and the discredit into which he brought that science by identifying it with the aggressive conceptions of Hitler's Germany need not concern us here. Under him and his disciples geopolitics became the prolific mother of a number of subsidiary sciences—grouped together as geo-sciences—including such strange conceptions as geomedicine, geonomics, etc. But as we shall see later Haushofer introduced some necessary correctives into the thinking of Mackinder and made geopolitics a serious subject of study.

Each country, as Mackinder insisted, has its own geographical perspective. We in India have so long been accustomed to look at maps based on the Greenwich meridian that we are inclined to accept the British view of geography as the only one. But one has only to look at the map which decorates the crest of the United Nations to realise how differently the world looks when maps are drawn with the North Pole as the centre. The difference becomes much greater if instead of the mercatorial projection according to which the earth looks flat, maps were made to emphasise its globular character. The relations between areas will be seen to be different from what they appear to be on a flat chart. On a polar projection the maps will not only look unfamiliar but distances planted in our mind will be seen to be different.

Since the world is a globe it is possible to consider any single point as its centre and make it, at least in imagination, revolve around that point. This national approach to geography has been one of the major difficulties of modern times. A second and even more complicating factor is that the foundations of geography as we now know were laid by mariners and represent mainly the sea-farers' point of view and reflect the achievement of the great navigators. The beginnings of modern geography were made by the navigators who explored unknown seas, charted new routes discovered hitherto unknown continents. The Diazes, the Columbuses, the Vasco da Gamas and the Maggellens down to the time of Cook were the heroes of the mariners' geography. But if you omit the new hemisphere and Australia and the islands in the far Pacific, these explorers were not reaching out to new countries or discovering new facts of geography. From the point of view of the landsmen, India, China, Japan and the islands of Indonesia were known to Europe long before Portugal, Genoa or Venice thought of taking to navigation. Across the silk road caravans had travelled to Europe bearing the produce of China. From at least the time of Herodotus India was known to the West. The routes of land communication were not only well marked out but the facts of continental geography were also fairly well known, as the successive conquests of large areas of Europe by the Huns, the Mongols and the Turks would definitely prove.

But geography as a world science is the contribution of the mariners, for the entire area of the world comes into view only when the poles are reached and the vast expanses of the sea sailed and charted. Geography had as a result to be a mariners' geography to a large extent. But it is well to remember that there are many aspects of this geography which lead us to have an unreal perspective about land. For example, from a mariner's point of view, the areas which could not be easily reached by sea, are not so important as places which could be so reached. Thus there are today vast areas to the north of the Himalayas of which our geography books tell little. And yet, the Mongols knew the geography of these areas well enough to lead expeditions into the heart of Tibet. There are again areas, which from the point of view of land empires, are strategically of the highest importance. To give one example, the Oasis of Ferghana has, at all times in Asian history, been considered one of the most crucial areas. As Toynbee says, in the Caravan Age it was the central point of the world. Its importance has by no means ceased but in an age whose views are coloured by sea power, Ferghana is but an unknown area in Central Asia.

Any student of geography, looking at the globe, could see that there are two kinds of wide open spaces, which may for convenience be defined by the common name of sea—the water seas that encircle the land and the sand, and tundra seas which cover the heart of the world and beat against populated lands. The desert girdle that circles the earth is one ocean of sand and steppe beginning from the Atlantic borders stretching across Africa, into the Arabian and Syrian deserts and through Khorrassan and Central Asia into the Gobi. Casting one's mind back two hundred years, one could see these vacant steppes extending to the Volga and even across it. This vast sand sea, was not unlike its watery counterparts in many respects. The oases were the islands, some small like islets, some like Egypt, big enough to be organised from time immemorial as a country. The caravans like ships went across these vacant areas, braving storms, sudden deaths and lurking dangers. The camel and horsemen rode the sand seas as the sea-farers in their ships sailed the waters. It is unhistorical to think that sea-faring established more contacts, or led to greater exchange of culture than caravans or movements across the deserts. In fact till the invention of steam ships, the sea traffic afforded less facilities for contacts of this kind than the caravans of the desert. Steam ships however did not weight the scales in favour of the sea, as railways came into existence practically at the same time and made land communications easier. It is interesting to note that the Baghdad Railway follows the roads that Cyrus marked out.

Viewed thus, with the spaces of the globe shared between the sand seas and the water seas, one fact stands out unmistakably and that is that *a rim land, watered by unfreezing rivers, by inland lakes, and by the monsoon, exists as a marginal area.* The areas around the Mediterranean, the great Oasis watered by the Nile, the Tigris-Euphrates Valley, the Indo-Gangetic Plain and South-East Asia and China stand on the margins of the sand and river seas. It is in these areas that civilisations developed at all times. Great agglomeration of people with settled habits of life, with ever progressing techniques of agriculture gave to these areas a stability which enabled them to develop into organised societies. When history comes into view, full three thousand years before Christ, these areas contained as they contain today, the vast majority of human population.

History may well be conceived as the pressure of the nomad—both of the land and of the sea—against civilisation. Those countries which stand directly in the way of these nomads are destroyed and broken up from time to time. Those that are protected by geography received a backwash and after a turmoil settled down again. The earliest known instance of this movement of nomads is that of the Aryans. Starting from the vacant spaces of Central Asia, they occupied Iran and not only over-ran but peopled Europe. However, when the movement reached India, the fact that it had to divert its course first to the Hindukush and thus lose a great deal of momentum, made the Aryan invasion a trickle which, while it left abiding marks on India, had to compromise with the local population and establish a new society. The battle of the Ten Kings celebrated in the *Rigveda* shows clearly that as a population movement the Aryans broke down on Jumna, and what spread afterwards all over India in time, was something that was evolved out of the contacts of the two peoples which may be called Hinduism. Again the Huns started on the same path. Marching across the vacant areas, they over-ran Europe, broke the resistance of the Roman Empire, sacked Rome and established monarchies and kingdoms in Western Europe. So far as India, lying away from the main route, was concerned, the Huns who turned this way had first to establish themselves in the Hindukush Valley before they could reach the Indian plains. It was not the main body of this vast moving mass that came into contact with India and the result was that while the imposing structure of Rome crashed under the assault of the Huns, their invasions of India's frontier were never more than passing threats.

A similar story is told by the movements of the Mongols and the Turks. The Mongols under Genghiz Khan starting from the vacant spaces of their homeland moved with irresistible force, destroying the Khwarizmian Empire of the Amudarya Valley, rooting out the age-long civilisation of the Tigris area and carrying their arms across the plains of Russia where their golden horde ruled for over 250 years. But when it came to the river valley civilisations, though Genghiz's descendants conquered China and his dynasty ruled it for two centuries, by the time China was brought under control the momentum of the movement had been lost, and it was not the barbarian Mongol but the very civilised Kublai who ascended the Dragon Throne as the Son of Heaven. To compare the developments in China with the fate of the Khwarizmian Empire or the legendary Empire of the Khalifs in Baghdad, both of which were utterly destroyed and rooted out, would clearly demonstrate the fact that the rim-land areas outside the main highway of the nomad peoples, though subject to pressure at different times, could never be destroyed by them. The Turks, again starting from Central Asia extended their empire to the West, established even a homeland in what was the classic home of Byzantine civilisation—Asia Minor. But successive Turkish attacks on India by Khiljis, Tughlaqs and others, while they established ephemeral dynasties, some times of considerable power, were not able to change the structure of population of even the Gangetic Valley, let alone uproot or transform the civilisation of India.

The sea nomads came into world history only in later times as the oceanic expanses of the world were explored and charted only at the end of the 15th century and during the 16th and 17th centuries. Till the seas of the world were known, the sea-nomads could not extend their power beyond the areas of their direct knowledge. Also while the camel and the horse could traverse the desert, watery expanses to be fully conquered required a technical advance which could only come with greater civilisation. But earlier history provides limited but very instructive examples of the activities of sea nomads. The most famous of these are the Vikings, the North Men who starting from their inhospitable homes, plundered, destroyed and looted every area of Europe open to the sea. A great English historian describes their eruption as follows:—

"During several generations Denmark and Scandinavia continued to pour forth innumerable pirates, distinguished by strength, by valour, by merciless ferocity and by hatred of the Christian names No country suffered so much from their invaders as England. ...... Their sails were long the terror of both coasts of the channel. Their arms were repeatedly carried into the heart of Carolingian Empire and were victorious under the walls of Maestricht and Paris .... Every country from the Atlantic to the Dead Sea witnessed the prodigies of their discipline and valour."

It is only in the 15th, 16th and 17th centuries after the oceanic geography of the world came to be fully known that the sea nomads enter the world stage to loot, plunder and conquer areas that lay exposed to attacks from the sea. There is however one fact which deserves emphasis. The nomads both of the land and of the sea once they got settled became the carriers of the civilisation of the marginal areas. Thus it was through the Turks and the Mongols that the Iranian civilisation spread Kublai was the carrier of Chinese civilisation to the marginal areas of the celestial empire The Normans after two generations in France became the champions of French culture. "That chivalrous spirit", says Macaulay, "which has exercised so powerful an influence over the politics, manners and morals of all the European nations was found in the highest exaltation among the Norman nobles", just as the Moghul Emperors in India became the embodiment of Persian culture and celebrated Nauroz with traditional festivities and popularised Persian techniques in art.

The interpretation of history as the pressure exercised on great civilisations by the nomads of the vacant spaces, which is a favourite one with the geopoliticians of Europe, is, however, only partially true. That pressure, whether from the sea or from the land, is only one of the strands, and that not even a major one, in world history More than three quarters of the populations of the world were at all times concentrated in the great river valleys of the Rim Land or the marginal areas of inland seas. It is in these areas that civilisation which represents history has developed: in Egypt, around the Mediterranean, in the Tigris Valley, in the Indo-Gangetic Plain and the Yangtse and Ho Yangho areas. While the nomads finally overwhelmed both Egypt and the Tigris area, as the first was on the route of the Arabs breaking out from their desert homes in their great westward movement and the other was on the line of expansion of the Mongols, neither India nor China, nor in spite of many vicissitudes the civilisation of the Mediterranean and the river valleys of Western Europe, was uprooted or destroyed by these pressures. On the other hand, the great movements of civilisation were expansions of culture from these marginal lands: the spread of Buddhism and the development of Gandhara culture; the growth of Hellenism outside Greece; the great movement which carried Christianity from the regions of the Mediterranean to the whole of Europe these landmarks of civilisation were unaffected by the invasions of the nomads from the vacant lands. The history of human efforts and achievement lies in these areas and while no doubt they have been subjected to pressure at intervals, it is a wrong perspective which sees in the invasions of the barbarians, the central theme of human history.

It was this wrong approach that gave to geopolitics the reputation of a psuedo-science, the suspicion that it was but the pliant and willing handmaid of national policy. Mackinder himself was in the main responsible for this false start. The crux of Mackinder's thinking is contained in the following paragraph:

"As we consider the broader currents of history does not a certain persistence of geographical relationship become evident? Is not the pivot region of the world's politics that vast area of Euro-Asia which is inaccessible to ships, but in antiquity lay open to the horse-riding nomads, and is today about to be covered with a network of railways? There have been and are here the conditions of a mobility of military and economic power of a far-reaching and yet limited character. Russia replaces the Mongol Empire. Her pressure on Finland, on Scandinavia, on Poland, on Turkey, on Persia, on India and on China, replaces the centrifugal raids of the steppemen. In the world at large she occupies the central strategical position held by Germany in Europe.... Wisely recognising the fundamental limits of her power, her rulers have parted with Alaska; for it is as much a law of policy for Russia to own nothing overseas as for Britain to be supreme on the ocean.

"The oversetting of the balance of power in favour of the pivot state, resulting in its expansion over the marginal lands of Euro-Asia, would permit of the use of vast continental resources for fleet-building, and the empire of the world would then be in sight. This might happen, if Germany were to ally herself with Russia. The threat of such an event should, therefore, throw France into alliance with the over-sea powers, and France, Italy, Egypt, India, and Korea would become so many bridgeheads where the outside navies would support armies to compel the pivot allies to deploy land forces and prevent them from concentrating their whole strength on fleets."

It will be noticed that for Mackinder the persistent fact in history is the pressure of the men of the land-locked area on the marginal lands of the sea. It should be remembered that Mackinder was writing as the representative of the greatest naval power—Britain—which had, by every means at its disposal, been thwarting, all through her history, the search of the landlocked areas for openings into the wide sea. In Turkey, in Persia, in Manchuria, Britain was blocking through suitable allies, Russia's entry into warm waters. Mackinder for the first time realised the limitation of sea power when ranged against a continental mass inaccessible from the sea. During the 17th, 18th and 19th centuries sea power operating along the coast seemed to hold the keys of power and Admiral Mahan's book glorified it to such an extent as to mislead European thinking for a time. The fact that dynamic political power in the 17th, 18th and 19th centuries was concentrated on coastal areas, and that the effort of continental nations under Louis XIV and Napoleon could be thwarted by the naval power of Britain lent colour to Mahan's view. It is to Mackinder's credit that he rudely shattered the web of this false optimism and pointed out that if the Heartland was once united and organised, sea power was helpless against it. Mackinder writing as an Englishman saw the danger to his country's position and influence in this neglected factor of history. It is however specially noteworthy that the danger which he emphasised was of a German control of the Heartland and not of Russia being organised or advancing sufficiently in technology and power to be a menace to the maritime powers.

Haushofer accepted the conclusions of Mackinder and German thinking on geopolitics, divested of the slogans of *lebensraum,* the right of the growing nations to change boundaries etc., was dominated by the desire to control the Heartland in such a way as to make Germany impervious to sea power. Her experience of the first Great War had taught Germany the lesson, that if sufficient space and resources were not available, naval power could ultimately strangle and starve out the biggest armies. So her geopolitics proceeded to justify Mackinder's assumptions by setting as its objective the acquisition of space in the Heartland, with the object of finally controlling it.

It will thus be seen that both the main schools of geopolitical thinking, that of Mackinder and his English disciples, and of Haushofer and his German disciples thought almost exclusively in terms of the effect of large land masses on sea power. The first as Englishmen from the point of view of maintaining the greatness of powers based on sea power, international trade etc., warned against the menace of a Heartland controlled by the resources of modern technology. The German school, proceeding from the same assumptions emphasised the necessity of organising land masses in such a way as to make them independent of sea-borne trade and impervious to attacks on the marginal areas. Napoleon by his Berlin Decrees had attempted it, a continental blockade of sea power. Kaiser William followed in the same tradition, but both failed, it was held, because they had not sufficient space, and adequate resources available only to the power which had the Heartland under control.

While from the point of view of the Heartland and the sea powers this view may be important, it is clear that it provides no clue to the history of the Rimland countries, to use Mackinder's expression, the states around the Mediterranean, India and China, who as I have tried to point out have been affected only at great intervals and that not in any serious degree by the movement of peoples from the deserts and the steppes.

Geopolitics in relation to these countries of the Rimland has to work out other doctrines, which are more closely related to their development. India and China especially, with their very considerable areas, with their immense populations and with their material resources—not in the immediate past but throughout ages—do not lend themselves to the easy classifications of Mackinder and Haushofer whose minds were obsessed by the recurring fact of the direct pressure of the nomads of the waste land on Europe. Their doctrines have but little bearing on the evolution of India and China and in regard to these countries their problems in relation to world geography have to be approached along different lines.

One general consideration may be added as a qualification. Geography is not what was just created by nature. Rivers can be dammed and even their courses changed. Mountains can be sources of energy Deserts, once the most formidable of frontiers, can be tamed by better communications, brought under cultivation by irrigation and even made to yield oil. In China, the Grand Canal from North to South performs the duty of an artificial river. The frightening gorges of the Yangtse were conquered many centuries ago to extend navigation up to Chunking. So geography while still the most permanent and invariable factor in history can be considerably modified by the efforts of man.

The most significant and revolutionary of all such activities of man against geography has been the attempt to conquer space. Before the 19th century space was one of the determining factors in the history of nations, not merely from the point of view of opportunities for living, cultivation and development, but of survival against enemies. Spengler speaks of distance as a force which has not yet been conquered militarily and politically. The experience of Napoleon and Hitler in Russia, of Hidoyeshi in the 17th century in China, of the Moghuls and even the British who took over 100 years to conquer in India, show that space is of the greatest importance in the life of a nation. The dynamics of space is one of the favourite themes of geopoliticians and yet both distance and space have contracted woefully in the last few decades. Technology has helped to make distances and space relative. Even the high priest of spacial dynamics, Haushofer, recognised that with the advance of technology space has contracted. German armies penetrated into Russia and marched up to the Caucasus and in Africa up to El Alemain. Motor vehicles and aeroplanes can now cover vast distances and a supply line from the West to Russia operated through the Persian Gulf across Iran. In fact, the importance of distance has at all times depended on the methods of communication. So in an age of jet planes it has a different significance to what it had when the fastest method of communication was a horse or a camel. Again, control of vast spaces has also become easier in an age of air power. These limitations however emphasise one point that small political organisations based on limited areas have become anachronisms. In the modern age they cannot survive.

I have already alluded to the importance of communications in the control of space and therefore of states.

From the earliest time, the states which had the easiest and best-organised communication were able to hold together large areas. The control of the Nile as the single source of communication united Egypt and kept it a great power for centuries and gives to it even now a unity which most countries lack. The great Empire of Darius was based on roads while the Romans as everyone knows were the greatest road builders of all time as their far-flung empire depended for its safety on easy movements of effective forces controlled from a centre. The Mongol Khans developed an elaborate system of communications which effectively controlled the largest empire in history and in their time annihilated space and distance as effectively as in any age prior to the invention of aeroplanes. The state of his communications enabled Aurangazib to fight a prolonged campaign in the Deccan and keep his armies regularly reinforced. With the introduction of steam ships and railways the modern integrated state became a possibility and now with aeroplanes, entire conceptions of geography are undergoing change. In the air age distances are measured across the Poles which was impossible in the age of ships. Deserts no longer hinder large-scale transport and consequently areas considered of no importance before have suddenly become of special interest to the students of space. Unheard-of little places in the hearts of forests and deserts acquire immense importance and become the bones of contention because air control also requires fuelling bases, repair centres, etc., in the same way as ships do at sea.

The conceptions of air geography are, it would be obvious, basically different. Ordinary mountain ranges are for example no hindrance to air traffic. The long group of islands, Indonesia, which strikes the marine geographer as an archipelago of large and small islands constitutes from air geographers' point of view a valuable isthmus, providing landing space, fuelling stations, etc. Areas which the sea could not influence in any manner, can be reached by bombers and planes whose ranges are increasing day by day. So the old conceptions based on the existence of a heartland impervious to outside pressure have today to be considerably modified.

CHAPTER II

INDIA'S GEOGRAPHY

GEOGRAPHY has been at all times one of the great and most regrettable gaps in Indian knowledge. Worse than even our lack of interest in things historical has been our utter neglect of geography. This is something peculiar to India, for both the Chinese and the Arabs were expert geographers in their time. They wrote not only detailed descriptions of their own countries but of others they visited or knew about. But we may search the whole range of Sanskrit literature for even passably accurate descriptions of India's main geographical features. Of the mountain systems that Indian books speak, Sumeru would appear to be wholly mythological; Gandhamadan is equally a vague definition which may be presumed to be the Tibetan Plateau. Only of the Himalaya, the most dominating physical feature of the country, is any detailed knowledge available in Indian literature. This great mountain range we shall consider separately. Compared to the knowledge of the Himalayas, or at least its lower range, the knowledge available in Indian lore about the Vindhyas, the Aravalli range and the Sahyadri—all of them indeed familiar to our people—is scanty.

States and kingdoms are of course mentioned but even about them there are but few geographical details available. Sometimes the details given are contradictory. The only great writers who show an adequate geographical knowledge are Kautilya, Vatsyayana and Kalidasa. Kautilya in dealing with gems and other products mentions the areas in which they are found. For example, he mentions the Tamraparni, Pandya Kavāta and the Churni river in the Kerala country among places where gems are obtained. Most parts of India are alluded to but there are hardly any geographical data of value that could be extracted from them. Vatsyayana, again, in his *Kamasutra* while enumerating the special customs and practices prevalent in different parts of India shows considerable familiarity with the geography and political divisions of the country. His general division, of *prācya*—the eastern parts, of *madhya desa,* central India, or *dakshinapatha* or the south, is not very helpful. He however mentions many states and shows a fairly accurate knowledge of their location. But his contribution to geography ends here, for though his references to customs and social behaviour provide invaluable data to the social historian, they are of little use to the geographer.

Kalidasa stands on a different footing. In his *Meghaduta* and *Raghuvamsa,* he shows a detailed knowledge of geography, of hills, rivers, plains, mountains and cities and describes them accurately. From Ramagiri to the Himalayan gate through which he asks the cloud to ascend, his knowledge of India would seem to be that of an expert geographer. The cloud in his passage from Central India is directed with an exactitude of geographical knowledge, exceptional for a poet, to keep to a route and the rivers, hills, dales and cities which lie on the way are adequately described. When the messenger reaches Bidisa, Kalidasa does not fail to mention, not merely the river but the caves on its shores. As Ujjain does not lie on the direct route the messenger is asked to deflect his course in order that he may see that famous city. In *Raghuvamsa* again the poet shows his knowledge of Indian geography. The *dig-*

vijaya of Raghu takes him to different kingdoms, the characteristics of which are described with a degree of knowledge that makes one think that the poet was familiar even with the southern countries of Pandya and Kerala for he talks not merely of famous rivers like Tamraparni but of lesser known rivers of the West Coast.

These are however works of literature and not of geography. Of books giving or professing to give geographical knowledge there is total absence in Sanskrit which is striking. Such geographical knowledge as can be gleaned from the *Ramayana, Mahabharata,* the *Puranas* and the *Katha Saritsagara* are vague and often inaccurate, though the last-named work strangely enough provides some data about countries outside India.

With geographical interest so wholly absent it is not surprising that India has up to date taken no interest in cartography as a science. While the Arabs and the Chinese produced most interesting maps, from very early times, India has been extremely backward in this respect.

Even today geography as a course of major study is neglected in India. Such geography as we are taught in schools is elementary and deals with physical conditions and political divisions. No attempt has so far been made to connect the facts of geography with India's historical evolution or to provide a basis for political thinking.

In terms of pressure on space India's geographical problem is different from that of European countries. She has no necessity to expand, from the point of view of security or defence. Her size, natural resources, her location in reference to oceans and land masses make a policy of territorial expansion outside her boundaries unnatural.

Kautilya defined *Chakravarti Patha* or the empire state as extending 2,000 *yojanas* from the Himalayas across the peninsula of India, and the idea of extending the territories beyond the natural frontiers of India was never a factor with the most powerful Rulers of India. It may be assumed therefore that the question of space never worried Indian political thinkers. *Himachala Sētu Paryantam*—from the Himalayas to Rameswaram—was their conception of India. Every ruler with imperial pretensions tried to extend his authority over the whole area. The *Mahabharata* in its present recension representing the political ideas of the 3rd or 4th century A.D. takes the whole of India into its imperial design. The Mauryas, the Andhras, the Guptas and all other monarchies representing the imperial tradition attempted to extend their sway over the whole territory. But outside the natural frontiers of the Indian sub-continent, they never tried to build up effective rule. Chandragupta Maurya no doubt extended his empire to the Hindukush as a result of his treaty with Selucus misnamed Nikator or the victorious, but we do not know whether it involved only a sphere of influence with autonomy for local rulers or was directly administered from Pataliputra. In any case, it seems to have been given up after Asoka. No other Indian King seems to have held territory outside the Indian sub-continent, though many monarchs of Central Asian origin from Kanishka to Shah Jahan held the Hindukush valley with their capitals in India. That this was an unnatural geographical agglomeration was again and again demonstrated when after a generation or two the extra Indian territories had to be given up in favour of India. So, one of the main preoccupations of European geopolitics, that is the desire for space has not the same significance in India.

Next to space what concerned the Western geopoliticians was the question of resources. The experiences of blockade and submarine warfare had taught the continental powers and Britain the necessity of having under their control the natural resources which will ensure not only food and other essential commodities, but raw material for industrial production and strategic material necessary for defence. The very conception of Heartland which Mackinder developed was related to this. His Heartland was an area which had not only ample space but adequate natural resources and therefore was not dependent on sea-trade and was immune from the effects of blockade.

It is a striking fact that there is no such thing as equality of opportunity among nations, because fertility, mineral resources, strategic location, climatic conditions, etc., are not evenly distributed on earth. A nation's greatness depends to a large extent on these factors. The continuance of its greatness in history depends equally on the way these advantages are conserved and utilised. Fertility of land, for example, may deteriorate in time, leading to disastrous consequences. A distinguished historian, Prof. Sinkovitch, has produced impressive evidence to prove that the gradual degradation in the productiveness of Mediterranean lands during the later Roman Republic and the Empire was one of the major factors which led to the downfall of Rome. Erosion of soil, deforestation, encroachment of the desert, uneconomic exploitation and other factors may easily reduce the fertility of the soil. Wasteful exploitation may cut short mineral resources. Generally speaking the endowments of nature are of as great importance to nations as to individuals.

India is fortunate in this respect also. Her soil is fertile. Though neglected for centuries, it has shown evidence of quick recovery under treatment. She is well-provided witl coal, iron and other minerals, necessary for industria development and has ample sources of electric power Even in the matter of nuclear minerals she is not, I am told, badly placed. Her major deficiency is in fuel oil and here also, there is reason to believe that her resources have not been fully studied. In any case, with ample deposits of lignite, the problem of fuel oil is not so serious as it was once considered. India's main problem is her food supply dependent as it is on the monsoon whose vagaries are notorious: but the experience of the last seven years has proved that with a considerable extension of irrigation, reclamation of land, protective measures against floods, and above all scientific utilisation of land, the problem of supplying food to the people of India from her own land, can be solved at least for the next few decades. But the problem does not end there. The population of India increases at the rate of four millions a year. Is it possible for India not merely to continue to feed the millions annually added to her population, but to feed them at more than a starvation level? Geographical factors themselves have no value except in relation to men. The problem of population, their standards of living, their mental and physical efficiency and their productive capacity are the bases on which a nation's life has to be ultimately built up. While therefore India may be said to be well-endowed by nature, her deficiencies in some essential respects are important and require serious study.

If unlike European countries India is not concerned about space and at least in the immediate future about resources, the geographical factors about India's structure have clearly to be studied from other angles, especially her internal stability, the integration of her large and ever-increasing

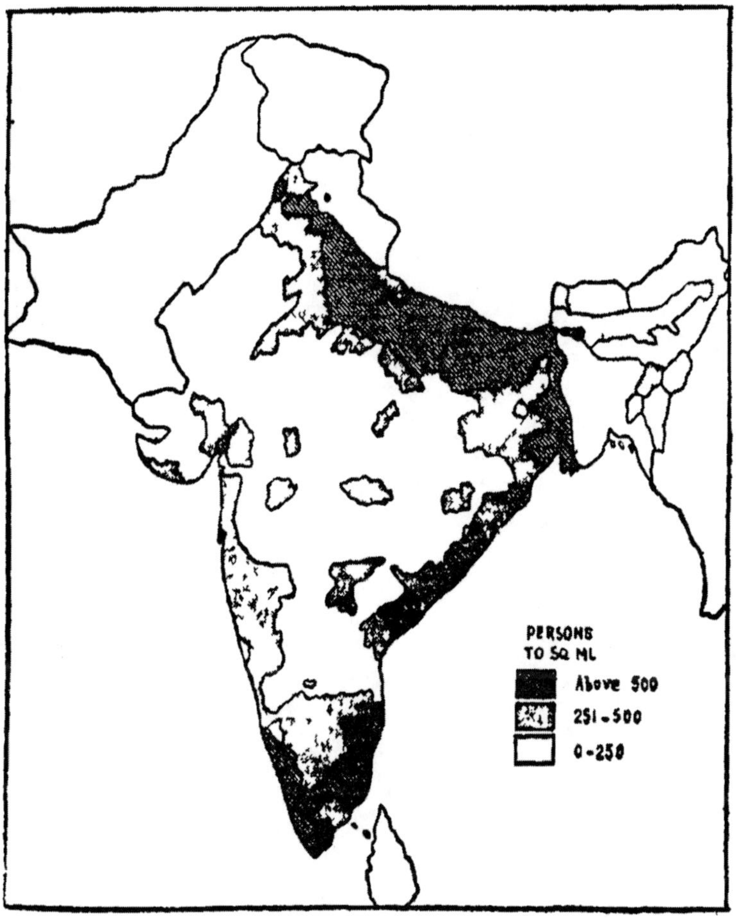

India—Density of Population

population, which shows wide variations due to differences in climate, food habits, etc., the closer knitting together of her natural regions, apart from a study of the influence of the two dominant features of her geography, the immense mountain wall of the north, the Himalayas, and the sea that surrounds her on three sides.

Now the land mass of India lying to the south of the Himalayas falls into five well-defined areas, the Gangetic valley including the Deltaic region of Bengal, the vast uplands of central India with its Vindhyan backbone, the Deccan plateau reaching down to Mysore, a desert area from the south of the Punjab to the plains of Gujarat and a coastal tract in the south expanding into a plain with its central portion drained by the Cauvery. For our present purpose it is not necessary to consider the island of Cutch, an extension in fact of the desert area, and the western littoral between the ghats and the sea which will be considered separately. The main area of India is included in these five regions.

A look at the population map of India will show that the concentration of population is in the two valleys watered by the Ganges group and the Cauvery. The Gangetic valley accounts for over 110 millions. The littorals and the deltas of the other rivers, the Mahanadi, the Godavari, the Krishna group, the Narmada and the Tapti account for another 50 millions while the Cauvery valley though extremely small accounts for 25 millions. The vast area which forms the interior from the Gangetic plains to the Mysore tableland is comparatively sparsely populated.

The first question that poses itself is: why is it that in spite of the existence of large rivers, like the Mahanadi, the Godavari, the Krishna, the Narmada and the Tapti which flow across India, population should be sparse and the economic development limited in these areas. The reason is simple. These rivers flow through uplands and not valleys, and do not therefore spread their fertilising waters on the countryside, till they reach the delta areas. The Godavari Delta is among the richest and most thickly populated lands in India, but the earlier reaches of the river flowing across rocky tablelands neither provide a waterway for inland navigation nor help to irrigate vast areas. The Ganges-Jumna system on the other hand, once it leaves the Himalayas spreads out its waters and covers an immense area of fertile land. Similarly the Cauvery once it leaves behind the Mysore tableland enters a plain which it waters and fertilises.

A second characteristic which is equally significant is that in view of the immense concentration of population and resources the Gangetic valley has always dominated North India. It is the dominant area from which not only political power but economic forces and cultural movements spread to *Aryavarta*, to the area north of the Vindhya ranges. The earliest imperial traditions in India were developed in Magadha and whenever a dynasty successfully united the Ganges valley it inevitably spread its authority over the entire *Aryavarta*. The Mauryas, the Kanwas, the Bharasivas, the Guptas, the Muslim Sultans in Delhi, the Moghuls—indeed the entire succession of north Indian imperial dynasties based their power on the Gangetic Valley. So strong was this tradition that the Ganga-Yamuna torana became the symbol of imperial sway.

Immediately to the south of the Gangetic Valley we have the Central Indian tableland with the mountain ranges spreading from Gujarat to Rajmahal constituting its back-bone. This tableland slopes gently towards the Gangetic

Valley. Till recent times it was widely and densely forested for we have it on record that the Moghul armies found the forests of Orcha so thick that they had to undertake a special operation to clear the way for them. With the upper Vindhyas and the Aravallis bisecting the area, the pressure from the Gangetic Valley is dispersed and finds its line of expansion normally into Malwa or Gujarat, and only to a less degree into Bundlekand and other areas which have thus remained outside the main currents of Indian development.

The dominant position of the Gangetic Valley which makes it the core of India from every point of view is so obvious as not to require any proof to establish it. That Hindu opinion always viewed it as such is seen from the fact that not only is Ganges the sacred river *par excellence* of India but the area from Gaya to Mathura, from Sangam to Hardwar, is recognised by every one to be the holy land of Hinduism. Every dynasty, even in the middle India, once it established its authority in its homeland dreamed of consolidating its rule by establishing itself in this area. The Satavahanas of Pratisthan, the Kings of Avanti and even the Peshwas of Poona realised that their imperial sway could be maintained only if they controlled the Gangetic Valley. The British advancing from the sea came to the same conclusion.

If the Gangetic Valley gave control of *Aryavarta* and led its masters to attempt to bring the rest of India under its control, the geographical features of the Deccan Plateau always baffled them, even if through overwhelming military strength, they were able to conquer it for a time. The unity of the Deccan tableland is as much an obvious geographic fact, as the unity of the Gangetic Valley.

Deccan is geographically a plateau commencing with Ajanta Range "where the ancient undisturbed rock beg to extend over the centre of the Peninsula right up to Nilghiris". This plateau, writes a recent historian, Hard Khan Sherwani, "is partly covered by a huge semi-circle ancient lava flow, extending like a ten days moon with of horn at Nagpur and the other at Goa.... The strugge for Berar between those who hold Malwa and those we hold the Deccan Plateau is explained by the fact that Ber forms almost the first of the lavaic crescent and is alwa the butt of the greedy eyes of their northern neighbours While the plateau ends abruptly at the Western Gha towards the east it slopes gently to descend to sea level.

The Deccan has always formed the great middle rampa of India and the Gangetic Valley was not able at any time to establish its authority over it on a secure footing. At the beginning of the Christian era we discover it as a flouris ing empire under the great Satavahana dynasty of Prati thana. How this dynasty which patronised the *paisac* language became in course of time the great carriers Sanskrit civilisation is one of the strange facts of history but one thing is clear that though the Satavahanas assim lated in time the culture of north and became its champion the Deccan area was not brought under the political control of a northern power. Even the imperial Guptas did no exercise effective authority there. Samudra Gupta in he expedition to the South avoided the Deccan tableland an his Allahabad Prasasti by Harishena makes it clear that he route lay via Sambalpur, Orissa and the coast. The Vakatakas held sway over the uplands and they shared wit the Guptas the Empire of India at the time. While the imperial authority declined in the Gangetic Valley, the

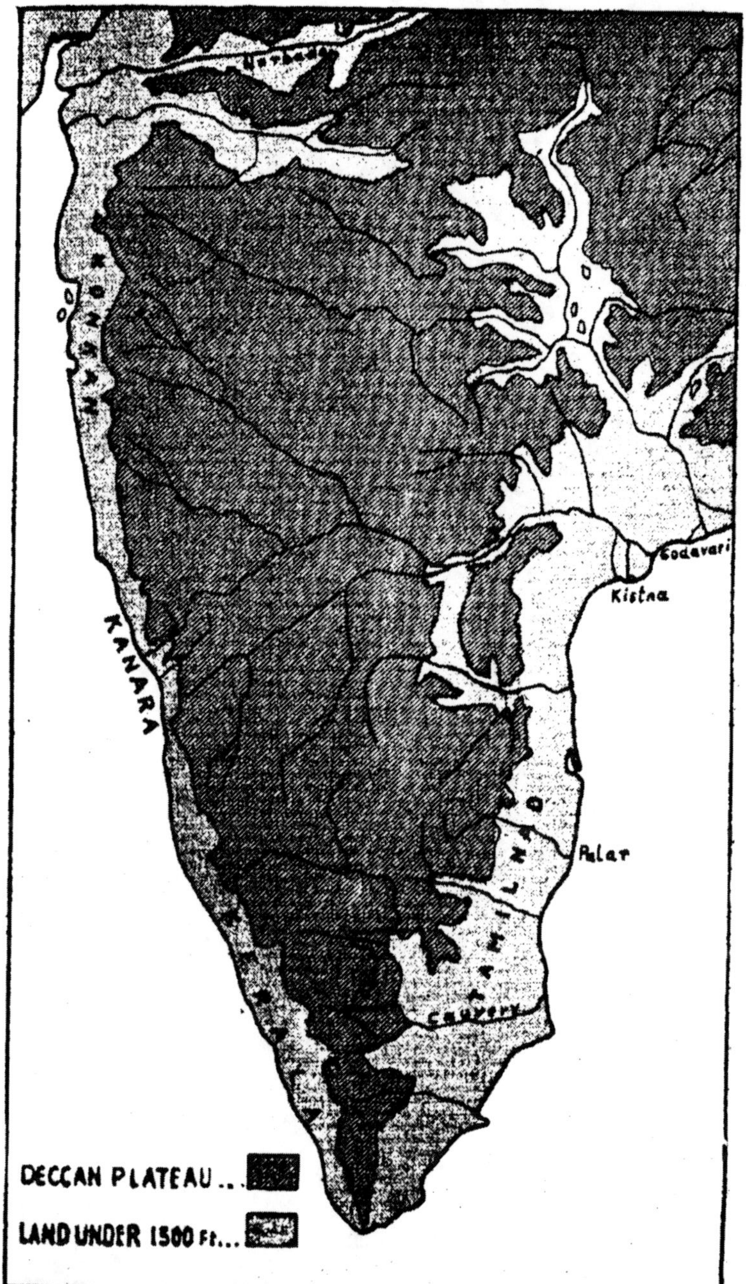

The Deccan and South India

Deccan maintained its territorial integrity under a succession of great dynasties.

The establishment of the Delhi Sultanate did not affect the independence of the Deccan. Allauddin Khilji indeed sent expeditions to the South destroying the power of the Yadavas of Deogiri and humbling the pride of the Kings of Warrangal. But soon the facts of geography asserted themselves, the upper tablelands of the Deccan being organised east to west under the Bhamini Kings, and the lower tableland being organised north to south under the Vijayanagar Emperors. No power in North India from the middle of the 14th century was able to challenge the independence of those kingdoms for over 250 years. It was only when the Gangetic Valley was again organised as a great military power under Akbar that the iron logic of history drove him against the ramparts of the Deccan. In the last decade of the 16th century Akbar opened his campaign against the Deccan Sultanates and over a century later when Aurangazeb died, the empire was still fighting in the Deccan. Technically the plateau had been brought under control and annexed to the Empire but 32 years after the death of Aurangazeb geography asserted itself once again and the tableland declared its independence of Delhi.

The Cauvery Delta, the core of Dravidian life and civilisation, remained equally outside the political control of the North. Its history indeed does not follow the course of events in North India, for, from the beginning, its activities were controlled by its peninsular character and were more orientated towards the sea. Hornell in his paper on the origin and technological significance of Indian boat designs has established the Polynesian origin of some of the backward races of South India and has also demonstrated that the outrigged canoe and the cocoanut were introduced into India from Polynesia. The excavations at Arikamedu have clearly proved, what was long known from Tamil literary records, that the people of the South were in close commercial relations with the Mediterranean peoples, that long before the time of the Romans their ships had sailed up to the Red Sea and the Persian Gulf, that intimate commercial and cultural contacts existed between them and the peoples of Western Asia and Egypt. From the fifth century (A.D.) the culture of the North spread, all over the region through the influence of the Pallavas, another dynasty like the Satavahanas, who were the carriers of Aryan civilisation. Kanchi becomes a great centre of learning, but there is no evidence of any substantial political relations with the North. The land policies of the southern Kings are only in relation to the States of the Deccan, the Chalukyas, Kadambas and others and not with the Empires of North India.

Their main political interests in historic times, apart from their local rivalries, were in Further India, in Malaya, Siam, Indo-China and Indonesia. The influence of the Pallavas in these areas is very marked and is now fully acknowledged. Again during the period of Chola greatness, South India looked across the sea for its political activities. A hundred years of overseas expansion and naval warfare by the Cholas are striking features of South Indian history which has no parallel even in the imperial traditions of North India.

Apart from the policies of Kings and dynasties the people of peninsular India were as we know from epigraphic records more concerned with maritime activity than with political expansion. Of the Nānādesis, the Valangai and the Elangai, an inscription in Baligami in Mysore (*Epigraphica Carnatica* Vol. VII P. 118) speaks thus: "Brave men born to wander over many countries since the beginning of the Krita age penetrating regions of the six continents by land and water routes and dealing in various articles such as horses and elephants, precious stones, perfumes, and drugs, either wholesale or retail". The Manigramam Chettis were equally well-known. Their operations extended all over South-East Asia.

The vast desert area lying to the south of the Punjab requires no description. It is in fact an extension of desert girdle, a geographical intrusion into India of the Middle East. This area is bisected by the Aravallis. To the west of the range lie the low lands of Marwar and Gujarat and to the east it is a highland consisting of Hardoli, Kotah, Bundi, Udaipur and Malwa. This was at all times an area of refuge, the geographical conditions of which enabled communities displaced by invasions to take shelter and carry on their life unmolested by the people of the Gangetic Valley. The Minas, the Bhils and other indigenous tribes first took shelter there. In more recent times when the Muslims occupied the Gangetic Valley it is to this inhospitable area that the Rajputs withdrew and carved out new states.

These are the five basic areas of India, separated by geographical factors but united by a common culture. Apart from these clearly marked regions there are the marginal areas which come into Indian history only in a limited sense. There are the tableland of Chotanagpur and the Chattisgarh States, still occupied predominantly by pre-Aryan and in many cases Dravidian tribes—an area which never came under the effective authority of the Rulers of the Gangetic plain; the peninsula of Kathiawad, which was effectively occupied from Gujarat, but geographically jutting out into the sea, and having dominantly maritime traditions and the Kerala littoral of the Western Ghats, a monsoon area of great fertility cut off by fairly high mountains with impenetrable forests and therefore remaining on the outer fringes of Indian history.

An important feature of this north to south division into three regions and of intervening tableland is the marked absence of direct routes of communication between the North and the South. Samudra Gupta, as we saw, went on his *digvijaya* along the eastern coast. The description of the *digvijaya* in *Raghuvamsa* emphasises the same fact. The pilgrimage routes also pass along the marginal areas. Nor are there in India any rivers flowing from North to the South or *vice versa*. The normal flow of rivers in the Gangetic Valley is from West to East as the land slopes gradually towards the Bay of Bengal. The West to East flow of rivers, in a country which lies north to south creates what may be called horizontal areas, and the geographical regions of the country have therefore less connection among themselves than if the rivers had flowed from north to south. In the Gangetic Valley, especially, this eastward direction leads to the integration of population in a closed area, bound together by the river and its main tributaries, thus converting the area into a dominant force in *Aryavarta*. From the time of the Kuru-Panchalas to today this has been the capital and governing fact of Indian history.

It is an axiomatic fact, but seldom recognised, that an extension of land towards the south, because of the change in climate following latitudinal differences, always creates problems of integration. Speaking in general terms, this means that an east-west extension within similar climatic conditions, leads to greater integration than states formed in depth from north to south. Climates vary, generally, according to the distance from the equator, with the result that racial characteristics, economic conditions, etc., lead to differences in social organisation which become persistent factors in history. The history of every country, viewed from north to south, shows this characteristic. Even in so small a country as Great Britain, the union between the north and the south, realised as a result of many centuries of effort, has not been fully achieved. Scotland remains persistently Scottish. In the U.S.A. with its great depth, the differences between the semi-tropical south with its different economy and the north led to a bitter civil war and even after the defeat of the secessionists, though the political union was re-established, the differences between the north and the south have not been lessened. In Italy, the political and social differences between the Lombardy plains and the south have long been recognised to be of a major significance. This is equally true in China. Though racially, culturally and politically united for centuries the differences between the people of south China and of the dry plains of the north are most marked.

These facts are to some extent exaggerated in India by the geographical factors discussed earlier in this section. While from first century A.D. at least the cultural unity of India was being worked out by the penetration of Sanskrit and of the Hindu social system, ethnically, politically and economically the three tiers continued to be separate. Only with the British conquest was the political, administrative and economic structure of the three areas unified. The Deccan and the South still continue to be racially Dravidian with the least admixture of the blood of Aryans and other races which penetrated into *Aryavarta*. They speak languages which though greatly influenced by

Sanskrit are of the Dravidian family. The unity of India that exists is based on such factors as the social and domestic organisation of the Hindus laid down in the *Grihya Sutras*, on the universality of the Hindu religion whose pilgrimage centres are spread all over India, on Sanskritic culture which attained an unquestioned predominance over the whole country at least by the fifth century A.D. But geography is continuously trying to assert itself and India's history can only be understood if we realise that it is a perpetual struggle to achieve a harmony between the Gangetic Plain and the Deccan.

CHAPTER III

THE HIMALAYAS IN INDIAN LIFE

THE geographical feature which dominates India most is the Himalayas. There are no mountain ranges anywhere in the world which have contributed so much to shape the life of a country as the Himalayas have in respect of India. It is not only the political life of the people of Hindustan, but the religion, mythology, art and literature of the Hindus that bear the imprint of the great mountain barrier. To the Hindus the Himalayas have been a perpetual source of wonder and veneration. To the peoples of the south, a thousand and five hundred miles away, to the men of the sea coast, to the dwellers of the desert land of Rajputana no less than to the inhabitants of the Gangetic valley the Himalayas have been the symbol of India. The majesty of the snow-clad peaks, visible from afar, the inaccessibility of even the lesser ranges, the mysteries of the gigantic glaciers and the magnificence of the great rivers that emerge from its gorges have combined to give to the Himalayas a majesty which no other mountain range anywhere can claim. The Hindus have invested it with an element of the divine: it is *devata*—a fraction of divine majesty.

It is the abode of the gods to the Hindus, not the friendly Olympus of the Greeks, but the inaccessible seat of the great *Siva*. From one end to the other, it is studded with sacred places of pilgrimage—Amarnath, Jwala Mukhi, Hardwar, Kedarnath, Badrinath, Pasupat and the rest and above all the magnificent and isolated peak of Kailas, the unapproachable seat of the Great God himself. Parvati, the consort of

Siva, the devi whose worship in different forms constitutes so much of popular Hinduism, is the daughter of the mountain god. One of the great peaks, Gouri Sikhar, identified in popular mind with Everest, is held sacred as the place of her penance. The holy Ganges takes its rise in the Himalayas and girdles it for over 500 miles before it streams into the plains of Hindustan to fertilise and sanctify its soil. The Jumna and the Saraswati, the Brahmaputra and the Indus and most of their tributaries on which depend the life of India, all have their origin in the Himalayas. "The massive heights of Tibet" says Owen Lattimore (*Inner Asian Frontiers of China*, p. 207) "dividing India from China also nourish the sources of the Yangtze and the Yellow River flowing into China, the Indus and the Brahmaputra flowing into India, the Mekong flowing into Siam and the Salween flowing into Burma." It will thus be seen that the central plateau created by the Himalayas is the source of life as of civilisation of nearly a half of the human race. Well might Sri Krishna claim in the *Gita:* "Among mountains I am the Himalayas"

In a very special measure the Himalaya is India's national mountain as the Ganges is its national river. It is true that on one side there is the great plateau of Tibet, but it is a thinly populated country, unimportant except for its size and mystery. The popular mind, not only in India but elsewhere has from time immemorial identified the Himalayas with India. The very description of India which has come down to us by tradition is *Himavat—Setu Paryantam*, from the Himalayas to Rameswaram.

The conquest of the lower regions of the Himalayas and the exploration of the great range itself must have been acts of high adventure in the dawn of Indian history.

When the story of India unfolds itself we find flourishing Hindu kingdoms already established in Kashmir and Nepal, both being valleys ensconced in the Himalayas. The kingdoms of Dwigarta, Trigarta and Madra in the sub-Himalayan regions are already famous in the time of the *Mahabharata*. In the story of Rama there is but little allusion to the Himalayas. It is true that the spot of Lakshmana's penance is in the lower valleys of the Himalayas, a few miles to the north of Hardwar, but the mountain range itself does not figure in the *Ramayana*. On the other hand in the *Mahabharata* story allusion to the Himalayas is frequent. We may thus presume that the Hindu conquest of Himalayas took place mainly in the period between the Rama story and the *Mahabharata* battle. The Pandava brothers at the time of their renunciation, it is stated in the epic, marched northwards and "beheld with heaven-aspiring hearts the mighty mountain, Himavat. Beyond its lofty peaks they passed towards a sea of sand". The holy lake of Manasarowar and the great Kailas itself, both on the Tibetan side, had become familiar to the people of India long before the Christian era.

The establishment of the great Hindu centres of pilgrimage from Amarnath (14,000 ft.) in Kashmir to Pasupat in Nepal could not have been later than the first century A.D. Long before this they had become popular centres of religious worship; holy men must have made their *ashramas* in spots where the scenery was majestic and life secluded, far away from the marring crowds of civilisation. In the period of the Rama story, the colonisation of the plains of India had not been complete and the great centres of *ashrama* life were in Dandaka and Panchavati—forests in the heart of Hindustan itself. The story of the *Mahabharata* clearly proves that *Aryavarta* had been fully colonised by that time and the *rishis* and *sannyasis* had moved to the more inaccessible heights of the Himalayas.

Gradually the entire range of the Himalayas, where human habitation was possible, became dotted with holy places. One of the most frequented of these, which attract thousands of pilgrims every year is Badrinath which is 15,000 ft. above sea level. Between Hardwar and Badri, there are literally hundreds of sacred spots, each sanctified by some legend and considered holy by Hindus everywhere. The extent of the sanctification of the Himalayas may be inferred from the fact that on the fifty-six mile route from Kalka (Kalika) to Simla (Shymala) every important point is named after a temple dedicated to the Devi.

The gorges and the routes across the Himalayas were also known and explored by that time. Kalidasa in the *Megha-duta* gives a description of the gorges through which the cloud has to pass to cross the Himalayan range and reach the mysterious city of Alaka, which mythology locates near Kailas. In the 6th, 7th and 8th centuries we have ample literary evidence of Indian rulers annexing Himalayan kingdoms. Bana's description in *Harsha Charita* of the conquest of Kashmir and Nepal by Sri Harsha shows that these kingdoms had long ago been incorporated into the historic conception of the homeland of the Hindus. This must indeed be considered an epic story, for it must have taken centuries of undaunted effort before the great mountain range was so fully explored, its habitable valleys colonised, its passes discovered and brought into use. All but the highest peaks, most of which have so far resisted even the efforts of mountain climbers equipped with the latest conveniences of science, had long ago been conquered by the Hindu explorers of those days.

The dominance of this great mountain range on the mind of the Hindus has only increased with time. Their epic poems describe its glory. The *Puranas* describe it with awe and veneration. In many of the legends they embody, the Himalayas have an important place. Two of Kalidasa's major works are dominated by the spirit of the Himalayas. *Kumarasambhava* is *par excellence* the epic of the mountain. The first canto opens with a great and thrilling description of the mountain-god and the magic of its presence is conveyed by the poet all through the major events of the epic. The *Meghaduta*—or the cloud messenger is no less a tribute to the majesty of the Himalayas. The theme of the poem is the message that a Yaksha, a resident of Alaka, near Kailas, living a life of exile on the Vindhyas, sends to his beloved through a cloud. It is through the Himalayas that the cloud has to pass and some of the most beautiful verses in the poem describe the cloud's ascent from the plains to the Himalayan heights. The scenes of Bharavi's epic* are laid in the Himalayas. The *Kathasaritsagara*—the ocean of stories—contains numerous passages describing the beauty of the great mountain. Nor is this confined to the literature of continental India. Wherever the Hindus colonised they took with them their love of the Himalayas. In *kavi* literature of Java: *e.g.* in *Smara Dahana* the same lingering admiration of the snow-clad mountain can be seen. Nor is it to be forgotten that the temple in which the King of Siam is crowned even today is known as Mount Kailas.

The Himalayan range, strictly defined, extends from the Indus to the Brahmaputra—a length of 1,500 miles. This is, however, only an artificial distinction. The two props, the Hindukush in the West and the Lushai hills in the East, are continuous with the great central belt to which geographers at the present time confine the name. It has

* *Kiratarjuniyam.*

an average width of 150 miles and within this enormous area the central range rises to an average height of 20,000 feet, eternally snow-bound, magnificent and majestic in its virgin whiteness. Rising above this huge rampart are the great peaks, Everest, Godwin Austin, Nangaparbat, Kinchinjunga and Dhavalagiri, mostly unconquered by human endeavour and challenging the resources of man to climb them. To the south of the central range is a second mountain system where the average elevation is between 12 and 15 thousand feet, also snow-capped and majestic but more friendly to human contacts and less inaccessible to pilgrims, explorers and *sannyasis*. Gradually they descend into another range, the outer Himalayas and the Sewaliks, pleasant, cool and finely wooded,. extending a friendly welcome to human effort and habitation.

"Even a simple topographical description of this multitude of little world Gilgit, Rupshu, Spiti and the rest would fill a volume of Himalayan dimensions," says Spate.[1]

Kashmir, the Happy Vale, Kulu, the valley of Gods, the Doon, with the sacred Hardwar and the hallowed *tapovan* and Nepal are but a few idyllic pleasances of this mountain continent, while the new cities which stud the lower ranges from Gulmarg to Darjeeling, the pilgrim centres of the modern age, are but her guest-houses.

Glaciers are of the economy of its higher ranges, primeval forests, rushing torrents and frightening gorges are of its towering mountains. Its climatology reveals a world of its own.

"These (the Himalayas) are" says an English writer, "the supreme mountains of the earth, tossed high in some

[1] O. H. K. Spate—*India and Pakistan*, p. 364.

convulsion of the primal age, and stricken immobile, a frozen ocean of lava waves whose crests are on the outer fringes of space, whose depths and hollows are the secret places of the earth unknown and inaccessible; rock-cut gorges set about by forest swamp and interlocking jungle within whose grim recesses life may pullulate shut off for ever from the outer world, Himalaya the abode of snow. At least 40 heights exceed 24,000 feet. This mountain continent makes its own variations of climate from the coldest, aimless arid heights to dark, steamy sunless deeps, glaciers whence torrents run through caverns, measureless to man, down to the sun-parched plains of India. Here the Ganges, the Indus, the Brahmaputra, the Alakananda burst smitten from the bound rock to wind a hundred miles through hidden valleys, subterranean gorges and leagues of treacherous Tarai marsh to spread their healing waters on the plains and so to find the ocean and the end of all things, reabsorption in the infinite, reincarnation and rebirth—the very symbol of the pantheistic cults that give them adoration."[2]

Geologists claim that the Himalayas came into existence as a result of the crumpling of the earth's crust. It is said that there is conclusive geological evidence that some portion of the Himalayas must have been under the sea at some far distant date. These are matters of scientific interest, but the essential geographical fact with regard to this mountain system is that it is the culmination of a vast elevated plateau, Tibet, the average height of which is 15,000 feet above the sea level.

There are two aspects of the Tibetan plateau, which are of great significance when we consider the Himalaya as a

[2]M'cintyre—*Attack on Everest*—pp. 10-11. (Metheun)

protective barrier of India. The first is the fact that the plateau of Tibet has as its northern boundary the Kuenlun mountains, in the west the Karakorum and in the south the Himalayas and the east is equally mountain bound. Secondly, its own elevation is above that of ordinary mountain ranges. The mountainous area to the north of India has to be considered strategically as one, a great quadrilateral, the middle of which is an elevated plateau of 15,000 feet above sea level and the southern ramparts an invulnerable range of an average height of 20,000 feet. The area enclosed is 500,000 sq. miles, frightening and formidable in its geographical features, an arid waste, windswept and waterless where trees do not grow—snowy steppes inhospitable to man.

In the Himalayas so far surveyed there are, we are told—

	74 peaks over		24,000 feet
	48 ,,	,,	25,000 ,,
	16 ,,	,,	26,000 ,,
	5 ,,	,,	27,000 ,,
and	3 ,,	,,	28,000 ,,

in all 146 peaks which are among the highest in the World. "This vast 2,000 miles of mountain sprawl," says M'cintyre "would stretch from Calais to the Caspian sea; valley, plateau and pinnacle, nature in her most savage and gentle moods, hot hells of steaming jungle lands, cold hells of the high reaches: lovely flower-carpeted valley, bleak windswept plateau, deep gorge where glaciers 1,000 feet thick have cut the mountain side like a *bruin*, ice ledges overhanging frightful precipices from which they crash with cataclysmic force, incalculable variations of weather and climate". This is the Himalaya.

But the quadrilateral of which the Himalaya is the southern rampart is something which no geographer has yet fully described—Sven Hedin's *Trans-Himalaya* gives us a graphic idea of this strange wilderness placed on the roof of the world. It was after 79 days of march that Hedin and his party came across a human being. The extraordinary adventures of that singular journey pass beyond the realms of belief: wolves howling close at hand, wild yaks charging, kaleidoscopic change of weather from extreme heat to extreme cold, sudden storms and equally sudden stillnesses, physical features which are enough to frighten men and 79 days of isolation. The following description of one of the days—not by any means the worst of his journey—may give an impression of what Tibetan weather is like. "We marched to the south-east in a strong south-west storm and were almost suffocated in the gusts of dust-laden air, which swept along the ground. We suffer greatly and cannot use our hands, the map sheet is torn in pieces and we wonder if we shall live to reach the next camp. Our faces are distorted and assume quite a different expression.......... The eyes are bloodshot and water, tears run down our cheeks, catch the dust and freeze. The lips swell and burst, and the skin round the nails cracks so that the finger tips bleed. At last more dead than alive we reach the camp. We hasten to restore the circulation but it takes time. By degrees our facial muscles recover their elasticity and return to their proper position and we regain our former aspect".[8]

This enormous expanse lies to the north of the Himalayas, inaccessible to man and beast. Its northern ramparts —the Kuenlun mountains—in themselves only a little less formidable than the Himalayas: beyond them lie Mongolia

[8]*Trans-Himalaya*, p. 197.

and the Gobi desert. Thus for over a thousand miles to the north Hindustan has a protective area which no other country possesses.

The English East India Company, interested as it was originally in trade and later in loot, concerned itself but little with the Himalayas. It was only in the time of Warren Hastings when dreams of Empire began to trouble the Company's statesmen that the Himalayas began to attract attention. In 1774 Warren Hastings sent Bogle into Tibet and the first modern attempt to establish trans-Himalayan relations began with this unheralded move. It was however the Gurkha War (1814-1816) that brought the British directly into the Himalayas. In the beginning of the 19th century the Gurkha Kingdom included practically the whole of central Himalayas, from Sikkim in the east to Simla in the west. The Hardwar valley and Dehra Dun and the area upto Simla formed part of this great Hindu State. By the treaty which ended the war the territories of the British in India included for the first time the Himalayan valleys of Garhwal and Kumaon and the petty rulers of the Himalayan States upto Kangra were "liberated" and brought under the paramountcy of the Crown. The Nepalese also evacuated Sikkim which became a British protectorate.

A period of notable activity in Himalayan exploration began with the acquisition of Simla and its gradual transformation into a summer resort of the Government of India. The Sutlej gorges were first explored and in 1818 Alexander Gerard crossed into Tibet along the route which was later on developed into the "great Hindustan-Tibet road." The cutting of this road, which is undoubtedly a great engineering feat might be described as the first attempt to connect India with the Trans-Himalayan plateau.

The "great Hindustan-Tibet Road" belying its name is but a bridle path, but it passes through some of the most difficult terrain ever trodden by man. It has four natural divisions. The first is from Simla to Narkanda. In the second stage it descends into the Sutlej valley past Rampur and again rises at Gaura. Then in the third stage, it continues along the mountain sides, through forests of deodar, crosses the Sutlej at Wangtu bridge and ascends to Oorni. At the last stage from Oorni to Pangay, a distance of 25 miles, the road runs on a height of about 9,000 feet. Today seven years after our independence a fair road connects Western Tibet with the Simla region.

The junction of the Sutlej and Spiti rivers takes place between unapproachable mural precipices. The boundary between India and Tibet at this point runs over the Lio Porguyle peak, which is truly one of the wonders of the Himalayas. The following is the description that a traveller has left us. "Even more memorable than the Kailas this inaccessible mountain suggested an inaccessible dwelling place of the Gods: a fortress shaped by hands, but not human hands; and if the scene was impressive by day it was absolutely overpowering at night, when the orb of night was slowly rising behind the dark precipice on which we midway stood. While itself unseen the moon's white light illuminated the deep gorges of the Spiti river and threw a silvery splendour on the marble-like towers and battlements of Lio Porguyle. It did not at all appear as if any external light were falling, but rather as if this great castle of the Gods, being transparent as Alabaster were lighted from within and shone in its own radiance, throwing a supernatural light on the savage scenes around."

The second major road across the Himalayas is the Leh-Kashgar route which used to be frequented by caravans from Sinkiang. The building of this road which crosses the Karakorum range was undertaken after a report by Pandit Manphul about the political conditions in Kashgar and the possibilities of trade with that area. The revolt of Yakub Beg and the establishment of the short-lived kingdom of Kashgaria awakened vain hopes in the imperial minds of Calcutta and Lahore and though the political dreams vanished, the Leh-Kashgar road remained an important trans-Himalayan highway until 1951, when Sinkiang was declared a closed area by the Central People's Government of China.

Before the Srinagar-Leh road was opened, the road to Chinese Turkestan lay along a bridle path from Simla, through the Kulu valley over the Roland pass and then through Lahoul over the Barra Lacha pass.

A third major route across the Himalayas came to be opened later in the 19th century, with the establishment of the protectorate over Sikkim and its absorption into the Indian political system. In 1886 a Tibetan force crossed the Jhelap pass and attacked Sikkim, but withdrew after an ultimatum was sent to the Tibetan commander in 1888. The importance of the passes from Sikkim was thus brought to the notice of the Indian Government. The result was the establishment of a trading post at Yatung, but the progress of trans-Himalayan communications was slow. Early in the 20th century the Indian Government under Lord Curzon forced the issue and the result was the Young-husband Mission which marched across the Himalayan passes and concluded a treaty (1904). Its political and economic aspects do not concern us here but from the point of view of the opening up of the Himalayas the arrangements concluded were significant as in addition to Yatung, trade marts were opened at Gyantse and Gangtok in western Tibet. Apart from these "roads" there are immemorial tracks along which pilgrims have trudged through ages to worship at Kailas and bathe in the Manasarowar. Also the Himalayan States like Rampur Busshair, Tehri Garhwal, Sikkim and Bhutan not to mention the kingdom of Nepal have knowledge of paths and tracks through which their trade passes across to Tibet. Annually over 12,000 Indians including pilgrims and traders reach western Tibet through various passes, a significant enough fact in considering the routes across the Himalayas.

The exploration of the lower Himalayan area on the Tibetan side was the work of the trigonometrical survey of India. Much scientific effort and skill was spent to trace the course of the Brahmaputra in Tibet and to map areas which had not passed into geographical knowledge. The names of the heroic Indian explorers who undertook much of this work remain shrouded in the records of the Department and are known to the public only by mysterious letters.

An equally important, if more spectacular development, in regard to the Himalayas which the 19th century witnessed was the growth of the great hill stations. Following the Nepal war, the area between Kangra and the present Nepal border, including what the Hindu public considered the most sacred areas of Gangotri, Kedarnath and Badrinath, passed under the control of the Government of India. Lord Amherst seems to have been the first to hit upon the idea of converting Simla into a hill station. This decision was important, for, from it stemmed not only the magnificent system of hill stations from Dalhousie to Darjeeling, but the exploration of the Sutlej valley already alluded to. Simla however did not become the summer capital of India till after many years. Lord Auckland and later Dalhousie used it as their summer residence but it was only Lord Lawrence who made it a condition that he should be allowed to spend his summer there.

Other suitable sites were soon discovered and major towns like Mussouri, Nainital and Darjeeling developed urban amenities on Himalayan heights. Well inside the mountain ramparts, roads, railways and other forms of communications had of necessity to be provided and as a result the lower regions began to be developed systematically. On the Kalka-Simla route alone, the intermediate stations which came into existence included such notable towns as Kasauli, cantonment areas like Dagshai and Subatu, sanitoria like Dharampur and lesser resorts like Solan, Khandeghat and the Maharaja of Patiala's summer capital, Chail. The entire area was opened up. Though the development of this area was considerably retarded by the fact that they were held in fragmentised portions by petty princes, they were gradually absorbed into the economic structure of India.

Wherever a major hill station was established, a similar process was noticeable. As a consequence, by the first quarter of the 20th century, the lower ranges of the Himalayas upto a depth of twenty to thirty miles, and an average height of 6,000 feet became integral parts of Hindustan, where an economic life different from that of the plains began to develop. From the borders of Nepal to the Kulu valley tea became a major crop. The Kulu valley became the orchard of India, its apples acquiring a fame which rivals that of California. The cultivation of potatoes and sub-tropical legumes became also matters of importance.

The only area, however, which was systematically developed was the Dehra Dun valley. This area which is enclosed by the Ganges and the Jumna is about 70 miles in length and 20 miles in depth and at one time the proposal was considered of converting it into a European colony, something like the Kenya high-lands. Lying between the Sevalik and the Himalayan range, and enjoying a pleasant climate and a varied vegetation, the Doon valley lent itself to development, as it was under the direct administration of the United Provinces. Road and railway communications opened up the area and its natural advantages helped it to become the centre of numerous institutions of all-India importance. The Roorkee College established in 1844 may be said to have been the forerunner of the great body of institutions which make Dehra Dun one of the centres of Indian academic life. The Indian Institute of Forest Research, the Indian Military Academy, the Doon Public School and numerous special schools for superior education have given to the valley an atmosphere of culture and research.

The 19th century also witnessed the utilisation of Himalayan water resources for purposes of irrigation. The Jumna Canal and the harnessing of the Sutlej and other Punjab Rivers made India dependent more than ever on the resources of the Himalayas. The economy of the Punjab and even of the desert areas of Rajputana became related to the flow of water from these mountains.

It is however only with the achievement of independence that India fully realised the inestimable wealth she has in water, electric power and other basic resources, stored up in the Himalayas: how the floods which now cause destruction and disaster could be controlled and made to fertilise areas, yield power and generally generate life: how rivers can be dammed at very high levels, as at Kosi fifteen thousand feet above sea level, and made to serve human interests, how the glaciers themselves can be tapped and how the higher ranges, so far only the object of awe and veneration, can be made subservient to man. In the 19th century utilisation of Himalayan waters, power played no part. The Mandi electric scheme (1921) based on Jogendra Nagar was the first attempt in this line. The post-independence schemes, the Nangal, the Ganga and Kosi dam projects have the generation of electric power as one of their main purposes.

Few people have realised to what extent the Himalayan valleys await to be populated and developed. From Chamba to the Naga hills there are numerous rich, thinly populated valleys, which except for the Dehra Dun area have so far been neglected. The main reason for this neglect was that this territory from the border of Kashmir to that of Tehri was, with minor exceptions, under the government of petty princelings, whose authority and privileges, a paramount power solicitous of the welfare of its feudatories, championed and upheld. The princes themselves frightened by the strength of the democratic movement in what was British India, were happy to exclude the penetration of their States by people from the plains.

The integration of the States following the independence of India has changed all this. The Hill States in the Simla region have been constituted into a Lt. Governor's province known as Himachal Pradesh—the Himalayan region. Naturally rich, possessing an equable climate, and but thinly populated at the present time, the Himachal Pradesh if properly developed may become one of the vital economic areas of India. An enquiry conducted by a distinguished American expert in 1936-37 on behalf of the Maharaja of Patiala, about the prospects of a sub-tropical fruit cultivation in the Kohistan area (between Kalka and Simla) showed that under proper scientific direction, every variety of fruit grown in California could be cultivated in that area. The valleys of the Himachal Pradesh are even richer than the Kohistan area of Patiala. Luscious grapes, peaches and peas go waste in the inaccessible valleys of Busshair Rampur. The rearing of silkworms is also possible in the valleys.

With the abolition of fragmented jurisdictions, the difficulties that stood in the way of active colonisation would now vanish. A suitable road system can connect the most inaccessible areas with the plains bringing economic prosperity to the population and opening up the areas for development. Natural water resources can be surveyed and made available for cultivation and the scientific methods of lift irrigation can provide ample water supply. The extreme cold which in a more primitive time made human habitation of these altitudes difficult can now be overcome. There is no reason why the spirit that colonised these areas in the earlier ages should not now receive the necessary impetus to carry the work forward and open up the lower Himalayan ranges and unite them with the life of India.

The *terai* lands to the south of the Gurkha kingdom are also showing the signs of a new life. The separation of the jute-growing areas of East Bengal from India has opened up the prospect of a valuable money crop for an area which had so far been neglected or reserved only for the amusement of the big game hunters. Also the reclamation of the *terai* has been taken up as an immediate project for the purpose of rehabilitating refugees from the Punjab.

The territories of Bhutan and Sikkim in the East and the undeveloped areas behind the Macmohan line are also likely to witness a new growth during the next quarter of a century. These areas, so long neglected, have now acquired a strategic and historic importance. Much effort is likely to be spent in the near future on their development, for the circumstances to be alluded to later render it essential for government to build roads, bridges and generally make the area a centre of activity in the years to come. To some extent, they have up till now remained border areas of mixed population and hybrid culture. Closer contact with India, education and the development of trade have already begun to transform them but a forward economic policy involving the construction of roads will also open up the areas for intensive colonisation.

It may well be prophesied that the next few years will lay the foundation for a major development of the valleys in the interior of the lower Himalayan ranges.

What has been the effect of the Himalayas on the political life of India? No other fact has had a greater significance on the evolution of Indian history. It had in the past cut India off from its continental affiliations. To the Hindus the world ended with the Himalayas. What lay beyond was the region of unexplored mystery, identified with the arid waste of Tibet. The great Empire of China was cut off from India by land for all practical purposes of commerce and peaceful intercourse. The repercussions of events on the other side of Tibet did not penetrate into India.

The ocean while it separates also provides the highway of commerce and contact. The mountain where it does separate, as in the case of the Himalayas, becomes almost an impenetrable barrier. In the result, politically India was isolated, from the rest of the continent and became introspective in its attitude. There was no appreciation of the point of view of other nations who, to the Hindus, virtually did not exist or were known only by distant rumour. The contact of cultures which renovates and revives, the free association of different peoples, which gives rise to an international outlook, and the interplay of political factors on a wider scale which helps a nation to understand the strength and weakness of different peoples, were conspicuously absent in India in so far as the countries to her north were concerned. With the great civilisation of China which developed simultaneously with that of India, the Hindus have remained strangers to this day. India's land contacts developed therefore only with the countries lying to her West, mainly Gandhara, Persia and Arabia.

It is a matter of significance that there has never been the slightest disturbance of social life by invasion from the side of the Himalayas. It is true that on one occasion, in 637, a Chinese General from Tibet did raid a few districts near Tirhut and then withdrew.

While it will be true to hold that Hinduism and the Hindu people have been saved by the Himalayas, there have been other results from the impenetrability of these ranges which have not been so advantageous. In the first place, it gave the Hindus and Indians in general a sense of contempt for the foreigner, which is the inevitable result of isolation. The rest of the world did not exist; if it did they were not concerned with it. In the second place it developed in them a false sense of security, a "maginot-line" mentality. They were surprised when an invasion took place, as they never looked beyond their mountain barriers. The strange fact is that while in all other countries the decisive battles that settled their fate took place outside their own territories, Bouvines, Leipsic, Waterloo, etc., in India the decisive battle has taken place well in the interior, at

Panipat. The reason for this phenomenon is obviously that India never considered her neighbours. The possibility of attack seemed distant to the Indians and it was only when the army entrenched behind the Hindukush marched into the Punjab that they awoke and began their hasty preparations. It is the Himalayan maginot line that is responsible for this attitude towards India's security.

Thirdly, India never developed a proper system of international relations. Her only immediate neighbour was Afghanistan which except during short periods was never organised into a single state. The interest in Persia was limited and China was altogether inaccessible. In the result, the great traditions of diplomacy which China cultivated in her relations with her neighbours, especially with the frontier states which continually threatened her[4] security were unknown to Indian statecraft. The history of China has thus a continental tradition: and Persia was, from the beginning of her history, caught up in the whirlpool of international relations by her continuous intercourse with Greece, Rome and Byzantium. A continental attitude of being one among a number of other states of varying power was not in the conception of Indian politics. The only doctrine to which Indian Rulers adhered was that of the *Chakravartin,* one who brought the whole of Bharatavarsha under one control. Where such a conquest was achieved and the unity of India re-asserted, they never entered into permanent relationships with states outside India.

If the Himalayan barrier saved India in the past what is its position in the world of today? Can it give the same

[4]See the *Inner Land Frontiers of China*—Owen Lattimore and the *Early Empires of Central Asia* by MacGovern.

service today when the political conditions of all areas bordering India are undergoing rapid changes? Can the immunity of India from the northern side be maintained in the face of aircraft which fly ever higher and fly ever faster? Are there any other factors which may affect the traditional importance of the Himalayan ramparts?

The whole problem of barriers has undergone revolutionary changes with the growth of air power. In fact, we shall not gain a proper perspective in respect of defence unless our geographical values are re-interpreted in terms of air. A land mass so protected by natural conditions as to be impossible of approach from any side by air, becomes an air island. Frontiers acquire new meaning. From the point of view of air a river frontier, however natural, has but little meaning. Vast stretches of sea acquire an importance, which in the conception of Mahan it did not. The airman's geography including definitions, distances, barriers, climate and strategic significance has become more important than the geography of the maritime era.

How is the position of the Himalayas affected by this changed conception? If the purely geographical definition of the Himalayan range as having a width of only 150 miles is taken—that is to say if it were possible to isolate the range and forget the plateau to the north—the Himalayas in spite of its immense height would not be an effective barrier. But the essential point about the Himalayan range, as emphasised before, is not its width of 150 miles, but the plateau behind it, which in itself is an elevation of about 15,000 feet and is guarded on all four sides by high mountains. In fact the vast barren upland behind the Himalayas provides India with the most magnificent defence in depth imaginable. No centre of dynamic power can be created anywhere near the ranges. The climatic conditions above the plateau are most unsuited and unfavourable for air operations and the distance involved from any reasonable point whence a continuous attack can be delivered on Hindustan from the Himalayan side is also an important factor. In short the Himalayas may still be considered a major system of defence for India, impregnable in the case of large-scale invasions and better than any man-made scheme of defence for so long a frontier. But no mountain range is ever a perfect barrier against every kind of invasion. While it separates nations and prevents normal commerce and intercourse between *peoples,* it has never been an insuperable obstacle against penetration by a determined enemy who has the resources of a powerfully organised state behind him. As we have noticed, the Hindukush has only been an ineffective barrier when Afghanistan and Central Asia are organised as powerful states. The Himalayan range though infinitely more terror-striking and fearful is also capable of being traversed by enemy forces at different places. Why it has so far not been penetrated for the purposes of attack on the Indian plains is not because there are no passes which open out to India but because the Tibetan plateau was never in the past organised as a great military state.

The fact that the Chinese were unable in the past to organise a strong military area in Tibet should not blind us to such possibilities in the future. It may not be a danger in the immediate future, but there is no doubt that an organised modern state in Tibet will alter the character of the Himalayan problem. True, neither the Himalayan passes nor the climate and resources of the country would enable Tibet to threaten seriously the security of its neighbours. No major danger to Indian defences can develop from a country, which is so sparsely populated and whose resources are so meagre. But the Himalayan boundary will no longer be the dead boundary that it has been since the beginning of Indian history.

For the future the Himalayas will undoubtedly become a major object of political and economic interest. The study of Himalayan geography, geology, flora, fauna and its climatological phenomena and a hundred other matters connected with its life has now become most urgent for all students interested in the welfare of India.

CHAPTER IV

THE SEA

NEXT to the Himalayas, what has affected Indian history more than any other geographical factor is the Indian Ocean. The following bare facts will show how greatly India is dependent on the ocean that washes the three sides of her coast. India has no ports except on the Indian Ocean. Over 85 per cent of the sub-continent's trade is carried over the waters. The raw materials necessary for her industries come almost exclusively by the sea. Normal communications with other countries, apart from the small percentage which uses air transport is still mainly across the seas. A great portion of her internal trade even today is carried by country craft from port to port along the entire peninsular coastline. The history of Peninsular India from the earliest days has been intimately connected with the Indian Ocean.

Of the great oceans of the world the Indian Ocean is alone an embayed ocean. For the most part its area is walled off on three sides by land, with the southern side of Asia forming a roof over it. The continent of Africa constitutes the western wall, while Burma, Malaya and the insular continuations protect the eastern side. The vital feature which differentiates the Indian Ocean from the Pacific and the Atlantic is not the two sides but the sub-continent of India which juts out far into the sea for a thousand miles to its tapering end at Cape Comorin. It is the geographical position of India that changes the character of the Indian Ocean.

Compared with the other oceans, this feature stands out most clearly. The Arctic and the Antarctic, circling the poles have but little connection with inhabited land. The Pacific and the Atlantic on the other hand lie from north to south like gigantic highways. They have no land roof, no vast land area jutting out into their expanse. The Pacific roof is at the end of the two continents, in the icebound zones of East Siberia or Alaska. Considered geographically the Indian Ocean in spite of the vastness of its surface and the oceanic character of its currents and winds, is more like a landlocked sea.

Another important feature of this Ocean is the distribution of islands and archipelagoes near its continental shores or in its vastness. Apart from Ceylon which is attached geographically to India, and Madagascar which is near to the African mainland, the oceanic spaces do not possess the same distribution of islands which is so marked a feature of the Pacific. Even in the case of the Atlantic, Iceland, the Azores and the West Indian Archipelago, not to speak of Great Britain and Ireland, constitute a geographical feature of great importance.

The Indian Ocean washes the entire African east coast up to Somaliland, the south eoast of Arabia, the southern shores of Iran and Baluchistan, the peninsula of India, the western shores of Burma, the Malay Peninsula and Sumatra. Its eastern and western entrances are guarded by two narrow straits, the Bab el Mandeb and the Straits of Malacca both of which can be easily controlled. From the Bab el Mandeb, the entrance is into the Red Sea, which being an inland sea is controlled by the lands on either side. The Straits of Malacca lead to the vast expanse of the Pacific, but here again the lands on either side become so narrow as to be easily capable of effective control of egress and ingress.

The main islands in the ocean are Ceylon, which is so close to India as to lose its insular character, and Madagascar which by its size and position provides an ideal cover to the South-East coast of Africa. Ceylon has at least two fine harbours, Colombo and Trincomalee, whose importance has been recognised from time immemorial and Madagascar has unique facilities in Diego Suares which the Third Republic vainly converted into a base second only to Singapore in the Indian Ocean. The other islands of importance whose geographical situation has to be noticed are Socotra on the Arabian coast, Zanzibar and Seychelles on the East African side, Mauritius and Reunion on the tropic of Capricorn. The Laccadives and the Maladives in the Arabian Sea near the Indian coast, the Bahrein group near the Persian Gulf, the Andamans and the Nicobars in the Bay of Bengal and Penang are the other island features which have a great bearing on maritime history.

The distances have also to be kept in mind. The Andamans are over 700 miles from the nearest Indian port and over 400 miles from the Burmese side. Mauritius lies 2,094 miles away from Colombo, while Socotra is no less than 1,000 miles. Penang is situated 1,278 miles away from Ceylon. The Laccadives and the Maladives, small islets dotted over a great length to the South-west of India provide no suitable harbour. In fact except Daman and Diu the Indian coast has no suitable islands near enough to afford cover.

The bays and bights of the Indian Ocean require special consideration. To the north-west corner is the Persian Gulf, a protected landlocked sea with Ormuz commanding the entry. With the valley of the Euphrates and the Tigris and the historic land of Mesopotamia as its hinterland this sea has in the past had a dominant role in shaping the history of oceanic navigation and may in the future have even a greater influence than in the past.

The Arabian Sea, a vast expanse separating the two peninsulas of India and Arabia and bounded on the north by the barren coast line of Persia, is one of the vital seas of the world. As a result of the seasonal monsoon it has been for at least 3,000 years a great highway of commerce and intercourse. The Indians, the Phoenicians, the Arabs —in fact all the seafaring nations of the East—have considered this to be the chief area of navigation.

The Gulf of Aden is the bottleneck which is created by the projection of Africa and the south-eastern tip of Arabia, the two shores running more or less parallel here and ending at the straits of Bab el Mandeb. The entry to this gulf from the east side is controlled by the island of Socotra. For ages it had been the home waters of the Arab corsairs who had their base in Aden, a covered and almost hidden post on the coast of the tip of Arabia.

The Bay of Bengal, lying to the east of India and separating Burma and Malaya from the peninsula of Hindustan is also governed by the monsoon. Further, it is said to be one of the four sea areas in the world subject to the phenomenon of revolving storms. From the ports on the east coast of India argosies have sailed this sea from the dawn of history and the colonisation of the Pacific islands by the Hindus shows the extent to which this sea had been explored and navigated at least 2,000 years ago.

The Gulf of Malacca is like the mouth of a crocodile, the Peninsula of Malaya being the upper and the jutting end of Sumatra being the lower jaw. The entry to the Gulf can be controlled by the Nicobars and the narrow end is dominated by the island of Malacca.

The wind currents of the area are specially important and are perhaps unique in the world in their effects. The monsoon whose regular action was discovered for the West by Hippalus in A.D. 45 dominated the navigation of the Arabian Sea and the Bay of Bengal till the invention of steamships in the nineteenth century. The south-west monsoon which blows across the Arabian Sea determined for many thousand years the trade route which the ships followed. Following this wind they sailed from the Arabian and Red Sea ports to the coast of India. Equally its flow into the Bay of Bengal and its return by the same route after a period of calm governed the sailing in that area also. Thus for a period of well over five months the direction and route of sailing were determined by these winds and the navigators of the Indian Ocean who had closely studied the action of these phenomena were able to make full use of them.

Allusion may also be made to the revolving storms of the Bay of Bengal, an ever present danger to shipping in that area. Another factor of importance relating to the Indian Ocean is its essentially tropical character. Its northern end does not go much beyond the Tropic of Cancer. Its land-bounded area is therefore free from the effects of icebergs and other oceanic obstructions arising from the frozen polar regions. Heavy mists, fog and other difficulties which prevented early navigation are also absent in the Indian Ocean. The rigours of climate are also greatly modified by the geographic situation.

The lack of well-defined "streams" like the Gulf Stream and its counterpart in the Pacific may also be noted. The importance of these streams has been more climatic than navigational and as such their absence has not materially affected the development of sea-going traffic in the Indian Ocean.

Partly perhaps as a result of the monsoons, and partly as a result of the earlier growth of civilisation, the Indian Ocean was undoubtedly the first centre of oceanic activity. The first naval and oceanic tradition in fact grew up in the lands washed by the Arabian Sea. European writers, ignorant for the most part of even the main facts of Asiatic history, have assumed it as an axiom that navigational tradition first developed around the Aegean. Mackinder for example states: "Modern research has made it plain that the leading sea-faring race of antiquity came at all times from that square of water between Europe and Asia which is known alternatively as the Aegean Sea and the Archipelago, the chief sea of the Greeks. Sailors from this sea would appear to have taught the Phoenicians their trade...." Perhaps he was thinking in terms of the development of sea-faring traditions in Europe, but in terms of world history this statement is obviously inaccurate. Long before sea-faring developed in the limited Aegean waters, oceanic navigation had become common with the coastal people of Peninsular India.

A recent writer has noted that the South-East Trade Wind of the Indian Ocean seems designed for the use of big sailing ships. "So are the other winds of that great ocean—the wild westerlies of the far south, the dependable monsoons which made possible the sailing commerce of the ancient East and still bring fleets of Arab, Indian and Persian dhows upon their voyages between the Persian Gulf, India and Zanzibar. The west winds could blow a square rigged ship from Good Hope to Australia in three weeks and less though the distance is 6,000 miles."*

It is not the Vindhyas and the tableland alone that separate Aryavarta from the Deccan. The main differentiating characteristic is the attitude towards the sea. To the people of North India, with their Central Asian traditions, the sea meant very little. Their conception of politics is well expressed by Kalidasa, who describes the ideal kings of the Raghu Dynasty as *Āsamudra Kshitiesānām*—rulers whose territory extended to the shores of the sea. The idea of ruling the seas, far less of ruling lands across the seas, never entered the minds of the monarchs of the north while it was a normal conception with the Kalingas, the Cholas and the Pandyas. This is not to say that the Aryans after their arrival in India did not become familiar with the sea or with maritime navigation, but to them population movements, political power, etc., were bounded by the sea. In South India on the other hand population movements and cultural developments would seem to have been determined by the sea. The prehistoric finds at Maski in Mysore and other centres establish maritime relationships with the West, the Arabian Sea coast and the Mediterranean basin, while the prevalence of Austric languages even today and the continuance of kinship systems among the Dravidian populations similar to those of Polynesians indicate population and culture movement from the Pacific. The prevalence of the forms of Austric language in the Nicobars and its spread not only to different parts of India but to Madagascar, where it was powerful enough to establish a permanent dominance, are evidences of large-scale population and culture movements from the Pacific. The Polynesian origin of the dominant

* Villiers *Indian Ocean*, p. 12.

racial groups in Madagascar is generally accepted now and a movement on so vast a scale could not have left South India untouched. In fact Mrs. Irawati Karve in her recent work which deals exhaustively with kinship organisation among Aryan and Dravidian races, establishes the fact that the kinship system of the Dravidian peoples, and even of the Marathas who have been Sanskritised in their language, bear striking similarity to the system prevalent in Polynesia. This, together with such other evidences as the introduction of the outrigged canoe, and the coconut, from the Pacific islands would seem to establish the fact that the racial and cultural relationships of South India were with the oceanic people even in prehistoric times. Mrs. Karve seems to hold the view that the dominant peoples of South India who originated in the Pacific were moving towards the north and occupying the tableland when the Aryans were settling down in the Punjab and expanding into the Gangetic Valley and the two peoples met and mixed only in Gujarat where she has been able to find surviving traces of the Polynesian social culture. The momentum of both these parallel movements having broken down long before they reached the Deccan, the two people seem never to have met racially, though in historic times, Hindu religion and Sanskrit culture attained a pre-eminence which gave a top layer of Aryanism to these peoples.

Sylvain Levi has pointed out that the sea routes to the East from the ports of South India had come into common use many centuries before the Christian era. When we come to the historic times, the maritime character of India's peninsular civilisation becomes even clearer. Early Tamil literature is replete with allusions to maritime trade. In a Tamil classic of the first century A.D. Kaveripattanam, the great port at the mouth of the river Cauveri is described thus: "The sun shone over the open terraces, over the warehouses near the harbour and over the turrets with windows like the eyes of deer. In different places of Puhar the onlooker's attention was arrested by the sight of the abode of Yavana whose prosperity never waned. At the harbour were to be seen sailors from distant lands". That this was not merely poetic imagery has now been proved by the excavations at Arikamedu. An extensive trading centre with large warehouses for foreign merchants has been brought to light where apart from other interesting things, dated Roman pottery has been discovered. According to the *Cambridge Ancient History* Italy imported more from India than from any other country except Spain. Pliny computes Rome's annual payment to India at 550 million sesterces, and the yearly loss to Rome in the balance of trade at 100 millions.

It is also necessary to emphasise that unlike the northern kings who were *Āsamudra Kshitisās,* kings whose territories extended to the sea, the southern rulers always proclaimed maritime dignities. Thus the Andhra kings assumed the title of *Tri Samudradhipati,* while even up to modern times the Zamorins of Calicut described themselves as the sovereigns of the mountains and the sea. From the ports of the East Coast a regular colonisation, as we know, was undertaken of the islands of Indonesia and of the territories of South Asia. Periplus mentions three ports in the Tamil country of which Kaveripattanam was the centre, as the places from which great ships which he calls *Colandia* sailed to the islands of the Pacific. Ptolmey also notes the ports to the north of Chicacol as centres of navigation to Malaya and the Archipelago. We have also the authority of the Chinese pilgrim, Itsing, for the statement that there were direct sailings from Negapatam to Kedah in Malaya. While there is no doubt that other areas also shared in this work of colonisation, the very fact that Chola, Pandya, Pallava and Malayala are names for tribes inhabiting certain areas of Sumatra clearly establishes the direct relationship between the South Indian kingdoms and the colonists of Indonesia.

That the political history of the southern kingdoms in historical times has been connected more with Ceylon and Farther India than with any kingdoms north of the Vindhyas is also a well-established fact. In fact both the Pandya and Chola kings were engaged in intermittent warfare with the Sri Vijaya monarchs for over a century and a half. The Chola emperor Rajendra in A.D. 1007 led in person an expedition against Sri Vijaya, captured Kedah and established Chola power on the Malaya Peninsula. Over 120 years later the Sri Vijaya king, Chandra Bahu, in turn, attacked Ceylon in alliance with the Pandya ruler. These facts may indicate the extent to which the southern kingdoms were connected politically with the states across the seas.

How much South India with its overseas commerce was dependent on the sea was made clear when the naval power of the Portuguese, represented by ships carrying heavy guns, appeared before Calicut in A.D. 1498. The mastery of the Indian Ocean passed to the Portuguese and along with it the trade of India within a period of five years. It is true that the rulers of the coast especially the Zamorins of Calicut fought hard for over a hundred years to keep their coast clear of the Portuguese, but India's authority over the waters of the Indian Ocean vanished from A.D. 1503, when at the battle of Cochin, the Portuguese admiral gained what in effect became a decisive victory—a victory more important in its historical consequences than the battle of Trafalgar.

From that time to the withdrawal of British navy from its bases in India, the Indian Ocean was no more than a preserve of European nations who held Indian trade and economic life at their mercy.

The control of the Indian Ocean and with it, of the trade of India, Indonesia and Burma was exercised by a very simple process, which the genius of Albuquerque designed and elaborated. It was by a control of the approaches to the Ocean itself that Albuquerque ensured the mastery of the Indian seas for the King of Portugal. He sealed the entry from the Pacific by the control of Malacca, from the Red Sea by the control of Socotra, from the Atlantic by his establishments on the African Coast, and finally he provided a base by the conquest and colonisation of Goa. As long as the Portuguese were able to maintain this system, they held the mastery of the Indian Ocean. When by the conquest of Malacca, the Dutch made the first breach into Albuquerque's system Portuguese authority in the Indian Ocean vanished and gave place to the rivalries of the great maritime nations of Europe, England, France and Holland. When finally with the departure of Suffren from the East, Britain became the sole mistress of the Indian Ocean, it is to the Albuquerque system that the British reverted. After the Napoleonic wars when the picture becomes complete Britain is firmly established at Aden, controlling the entrance into and exit from the Red Sea, at Singapore, guarding the narrow straits connecting the Pacific with the Indian Ocean, in the Cape Colony, able to intercept any European power venturing to threaten her authority. The strategy of Albuquerque found its culmination in the policy of the British Empire in the 19th century.

When it broke down, it was again because a power operating from the Pacific was able to break the defences of Singapore. The Japanese by conquering Malaya and Singapore entered the Indian Ocean for a short period, demonstrating thereby that the period of the domination of the Indian Ocean from the Atlantic was over.

It is, however, well to remember that the land powers of Europe sought more than once to enter the Indian Ocean by other routes. The first attempt in this direction was by Imperial Germany under William II. William evolved the grandiose scheme of a direct entry from the side of land into the Persian Gulf. His project was to connect Berlin with Baghdad by a direct rail route. The Berlin-Baghdad Railway was thus a historic reply to Vasco da Gama's achievement, the attempt of the land power to out-flank the sea. It short-circuited both the Atlantic and the Mediterranean and gave entry into the Indian Ocean in a manner which could set at nought the carefully planned controls of Albuquerque's strategy, inherited and perfected by the British. But the scheme was never fulfilled because the British, alive to the danger of their power in India, were able to checkmate it in time.

A second and equally grandiose attempt was by Mussolini, the successor to the pretensions of the Venetians, to destroy whose monopoly the Portuguese, inheriting the transition from Genoa, had sailed round the Cape. With a large land empire in Abyssinia, Mussolini thought he could meet the challenge of sea power and reach the Indian Ocean direct. If the Italian Somaliland and Abyssinia could be joined up Italy would have entered the Indian Ocean in force. But the war came too soon and Mussolini's dream turned finally into a nightmare.

From the point of view of India the control of the Arabian Sea from across the African coast remains a possibility. The European powers who have colonies on the sea coast may in time become independent powers and develop considerable naval strength. A new European-dominated state in Kenya, the Central African federation and other political growths of which we see the beginnings today, apart from South Africa itself, may introduce new factors in Indian Ocean policies. The eclipse of old powers, and the weakening of old conceptions should not lead us to the facile assumption that the Indian Ocean will remain isolated in future from the main currents of world politics.

The short period of Japanese supremacy in the Indian Seas following her capture of Singapore and the occupation of the Andamans demonstrated that the threat to the ocean from the side of the Pacific is a real one. Till the end of the 19th century the Pacific was not one of the vital centres of sea power. The end of the first war marked a definite shift of interest. The Washington Conference on the Limitation of Naval Armament in the Pacific was the visible expression of this change. Today the Pacific is a potential area of naval rivalry, though the Japanese challenge has been for the time eliminated. But we shall be making a great mistake if we think that the Pacific has been abandoned by the other Asian powers to the U.S.A. Few people remember that the Chinese Navy under Cheng Ho in the 15th century controlled the Pacific Mediterranean and his ships even sailed the Indian Ocean on commercial expeditions. The development of a combined Sino-Soviet navy based on Port Arthur may not immediately involve a challenge to American supremacy, but once the industrial potential of the Chinese Republic is fully harnessed, there is nothing to prevent her from claiming her place in the Pacific sun. India's area of interest in the past (under the British) extended only to Aden in the West and Singapore in the East. With the Pacific in storm the whole issue requires careful reconsideration.

It is outside my present purpose to discuss in any detail the effect of 450 years of European control of our seas. Those who are interested in the subject may read it in my *Asia and Western Dominance* which tries to give a connected picture of the political, economic and cultural effects of that control. For our purpose I shall state my point of view in a few propositions which have special relevance to the present subject:

(i) The control of the sea by a foreign power changes the economic structure of India, no doubt slowly but effectively. India's trade, unlike that of China, was at all times predominantly maritime. In China it followed the caravan route, the route of the camels. Chinese economy was therefore continental. India on the other hand, her land mass closed on three sides by mountains, had her trade mainly along sea routes. When these sea routes came to be controlled by the European powers, the economy of India began to be dependent to a large extent on the foreign merchants. When in the 18th and 19th centuries commerce developed on a world scale, the emphasis in India shifted from the interior to the coast and the great cities of Calcutta, Bombay and Madras began to take the place of Delhi, Agra and Allahabad. The development of her internal communications in the 19th century, mainly with a view to bring the produce of the Gangetic Valley to the coast, the neglect of the vast area of the interior untouched by those rail-roads, the maintenance of a fuedal system of indirect government over large areas mainly in the tracts away from the coast, the discouragement of industrial development, the creation of an indigenous subsidiary financial class operating over the whole of India from their headquarters at the port cities and acting as agents and distributors of foreign commerce, the ruin of the native industry of India—these were the results of the control of the sea which Britain came finally to exercise in the 18th and 19th centuries.

(ii) While naval power was helpless against organised states, the history of India from A.D. 1500 to the time of the British conquest, clearly demonstrated the fact that the most organised land power was unable to protect its interests on the sea against maritime powers. Akbar at the height of his power could not afford protection to the Mecca pilgrims. Even the imperial ships could not proceed to the holy city unless provided with Portuguese passes. Whenever the lords of the sea, whether the Portuguese, the Dutch or the British tried to defy the empire on land, not only the Moghuls, but even the small rulers of the coastal states were able to teach them a lesson, as in the case of Aphonso Albuquerque at Calicut or the British factories in Bengal when they defied Shah Jehan, or the Dutch in their final fight with Travancore. But where the land power became weak or was torn by dissensions, naval power was able to consolidate and expand and finally even to conquer the land masses.

(iii) Sea power is ubiquitous. Mahan the prophet of indivisible sea took as his text the quotation from Genesis: "And God said, let waters be gathered in one place". The oneness of the sea is an obvious geographical fact and its importance to an area like India, exposed on three sides to pressure from the sea, need not be emphasised. In respect of land power proximity is a major consideration. The Roman Empire was the most powerful military state in its day, but it presented no threat to India. Neither the Hans nor the Tangs in the days of their greatest expansion thought of a conquest of India. Distance and geographical barriers effectively control land empires. Distance, however, is no bar to the expansion of naval power. Portugal with hardly three million people at the time was able, from her distant base, to control the Indian Ocean and monopolise the Asian trade. Britain with hardly twenty million people was able to undertake a conquest of India, from her bases in the North Sea half way across the world.

(iv) Conquest of a country by a sea power differs from conquest by a land power. It is a significant fact that though large portions of North India were conquered many times by foreigners, India was never in the past ruled by a monarch who did not have his capital in India—except when it came to the naval power of the British. The Kushans, the Huns, the Turks and the Moghuls conquered many portions of North India, but their empire was in India. Kanishka ruled from Peshawar and his successor in the third generation became Vasudeva. The Huns, Mihiragula and Toramana, came from outside, but even when they oppressed the country and pillaged the people, they became Indians with no interests outside the country. The Khiljis and the Tughlaks have been absorbed in the population of India. The Moghuls, once they settled in Agra, lost their contacts with Central India and became a national monarchy. In her long history, the British are the only people who ruled India from a distant capital and treated India as a subordinate part of a larger whole. In fact the only foreigners who ruled India were the British. If this position is examined, it will be seen, that the indivisibility of the sea and the ubiquitousness of naval power were responsible for the long domination of India from London. This simple fact has lessons for us which we shall discuss later.

CHAPTER V

ROUTES OF INVASION

LIKE every other country in the world, India had been subjected to many invasions. Some of these were the results of large-scale population movements, while others were the military action of ambitious generals. Of the latter, the most notable examples are the raid of the Macedonian Alexander into the Persian satrapy in the Punjab, of Timurlane and of Nadir Shah, all isolated but spectacular incidents, leaving no doubt, confusion and chaos behind them, but without permanent effects on the country. The invasions which were the results of population movements stand in a different category. They change the nature of the population, introduce new factors into the civilisation of the country, displace existing social groups—in short they are revolutionary in their character. Some of these movements which have a direct bearing on the growth of Indian life have now to be considered in terms of India's geography. The first movement of populations of which we have definite and sufficient evidence is that of the Aryans. The earlier movement of Alpine race into India across Baluchistan which is postulated by many scholars is too vague for us to draw any conclusions from it. Nor is it possible to speak with authority about the Polynesian movement which is said to have peopled South India. All that we can say is that there might have been such movements but we know very little about them. About the Aryans the position is different, because this movement produced an outstanding literary monument in the *Rig Veda*. The *Rig Veda Samhita* is looked upon by the Hindus mainly as a religious book to which they fondly trace the origins of their metaphysics and their philosophy. But to the historian and to the student of geography it is a unique collection of documents, covering a period of many centuries, dealing with the geography, the history and the economics of the penetration of the Aryans into the Punjab from the Kabul Valley. When it ends they are in the Ganga-Yamuna Doab. The celebrated hymn to the Rivers (X.6.7) in the *Rig Veda* sings thus—

"Accept this my praise, Ganga, Yamuna, Saraswati, Shutudri, Parushni, Maruvriddha with Asikni, and Vitasta, listen Ayikiya with Sushoma."

Of the rivers to the East of the Doab, that is the Kuru Panchala country, the Aryans have knowledge only of Sarayu and it is doubtful whether the Sarayu alluded to is the river which flows near Ayodhya. What is more interesting is that long before the end of the Vedic period the momentum of the population movement had already weakened. The Aryans in the Doab and those in the Punjab, perhaps stiffened by new comers, were at logger heads. In the battle of Parushni celebrated in the 7th Mandala of the *Rig Veda* Anuvaka II (VII 2.1) the dwellers on the Yamuna and Tritsus, under the leadership of Sudas, are said to have destroyed over sixty thousand of their enemies among whom were the followers of Turvasa, son of Yadu, and Bheda, the turbulent chief. Also we come across allusions to Aryan enemies, for example in *Rig Veda,* VI-3. 10, where it is said—"Thou, hero Indra, destroyed both classes of enemies, both Dasa and Arya adversaries."

With the battle of the Ten Kings, the Aryan invasion may be said to have come to an end. The earlier colonists in the Kuru Panchala territory with the help of indigenous local rulers had fought and destroyed the attacking Aryans and finally put a stop to the invasions. It is notable that in this hymn, Indra, the great god, the Wielder of the Thunderbolt, the destroyer of the walled towns, is not on the side of the invaders but on the side of Sudas and his allies.

The battle of the Ten Kings is one of the greatest events in history, an event which indelibly stamped its influence on India and shaped the future course of Indian development. It may well be claimed to have laid the foundation of Indian and Hindu civilisation for here it was that the synthesis of neo-Aryanism, which we describe as Hinduism was laid. The Aryan racial strain became thinner and thinner while the neo-Aryan civilisation spread to the Indo-Gangetic Valley. By the time it reached Bihar, it had practically ceased to exist. Even in the Indo-Gangetic Valley where neo-Aryanism or Hinduism became predominant, the population consisted mainly of indigenous tribes as is well established by the fact that even a thousand years afterwards, it continued to be peopled by tribes which were only imperfectly Aryanised.

That neo-Aryanism or Hinduism, as we may now call it, was the outcome of a synthesis between the pastoral Aryans and the indigenous people may be shown by instancing two well-known facts which form the basis of the new religion. The *Aitreya Brahmana* which is the most significant supplement to the *Rig Veda* was, it is recognised, the work of a man who was the son of an Aryan Rishi by an indigenous woman—an offspring whom he refused to instruct in sacred knowledge. Even more significant is the fact that the arrangement of the Vedas into Samhitas was the work of Badarayana known as the black whose mother equally was an aboriginal. The inter-mixture of races at the level of the priests themselves had become a major fact, before the Vedic period had ended.

The Neo-Aryans spread not only in the Gangetic Valley but also made their way slowly to the plains of Malwa and Gujarat, leaving the interior to the aboriginal races. But in Gujarat though they were able to impose their culture, the Aryan racial strain was almost negligible as the recent head measurements by anthropologists and examination of kinship organisations by Mrs. Irawati Karve have clearly demonstrated. For centuries neo-Aryanism did not reach the Deccan Plateau at all.

The distribution of the indigenous races even today in the uplands of South Bihar and in the eastern areas of Madhya Pradesh, and the persistence of the Bhils in the Aravalli and Vindhya ranges show that as a population movement the Aryan invasion ceased to have any momentum after it reached the Gangetic Valley. The gradual spread of Hinduism all over India and with it the Aryan speech should not blind us to the fact that even in North India, outside the Punjab, the Aryans contributed only a racial strain. In Gujarat and in Maharashtra the neo-Aryans were able to impose their language but in the Deccan and in the South, the Dravidian speech not only held its own but was able to drive out the Austric and other linguistic elements. The spread of Aryanism and Sanskrit to the South, originally associated with Agastya's crossing of the Vindhyas, became an accomplished fact only in the first centuries of the Christian era, as may be seen from the earlier Paishachi tradition of the Satavahana Emperors of Pratisthan.

The Aryan invasion was the first known and the greatest of all invasions of India and we have seen that its racial effects were not very considerable outside the Punjab. The next invasion of which we have some knowledge was of the Achamedian Kings of Persia. It merely annexed to the Persian Empire the trans-Beas areas of the Punjab and had little influence on even the Indo-Gangetic Plain, except in the realm of art and architecture. Alexander's raid was into the Indian satrapies of the Persian King and was insignificant in every way, except in the eyes of the Europeans who pretended to see in it an early version of an alleged European conquest of India.

The really significant movement of which we have any information after the eruption of the Aryans is that of the Yue-chi. This was a barbarian tribe who had their homes in the vacant belt of Koarsu and Sinking in Chinese Turkestan and were driven from their homes by the Hun conqueror. They in turn drove the Sakas before them and in the first century B.C. the Sakas descended on India, through the Bolan Pass and occupied Sindh and from there it would seem threatened Ujjain itself, as the Arabs tried to do at a later time. Their defeat and expulsion in 57 B.C. was according to Hindu tradition the achievement of Vikramaditya of Ujjain, who to commemorate this fact established the Vikram Samvat era. But though the Sakas were driven off, the Yue-chi who had settled down in the valleys of the Hindu Kush began to make their power felt on India. Under Kanishka, their empire extended to Mathura.

The Yue-chi had arrived in the Hindu Kush valley as a result of the pressure from behind. But during their settlement in that area, the pressure relaxed and the Kushans as they now came to be called became a settled people. The empire of Kanishka was therefore a political

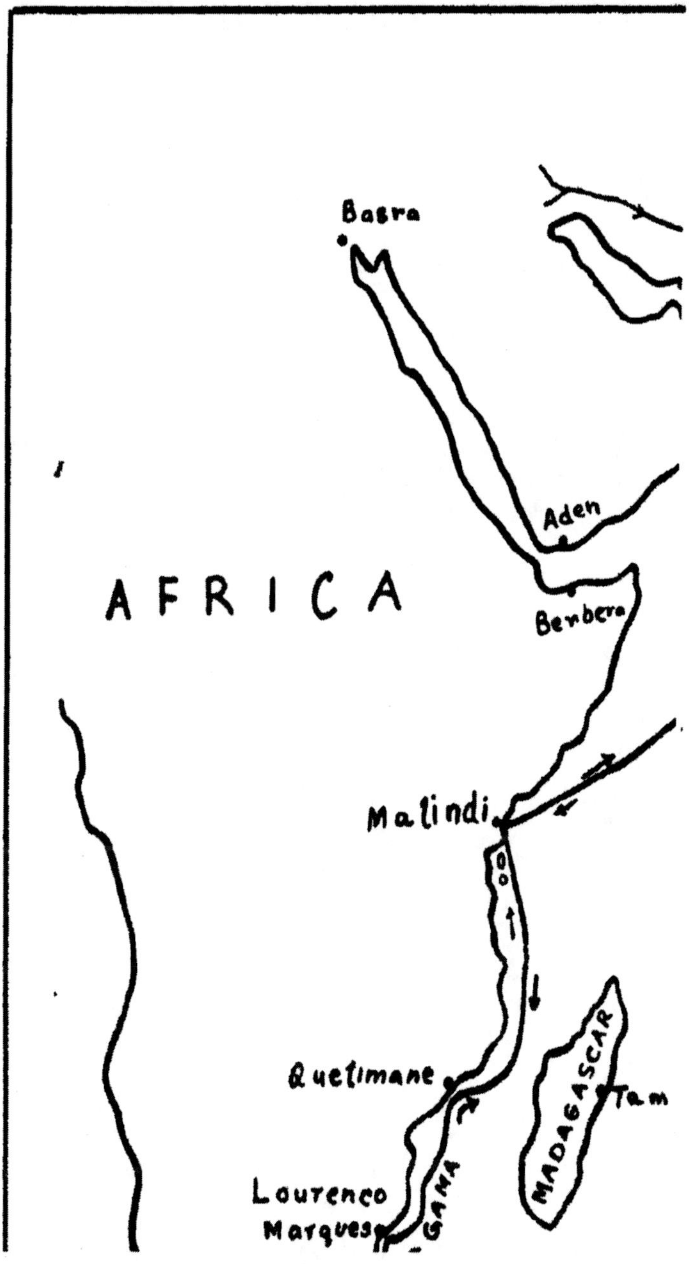

Owing to the book's antiquity and rarity, this map has damaged, thereby affecting the legibility of the original text.

phenomenon of an ephemeral character and not a population movement involving great and revolutionary changes.

The Hun invasion was of a different character. It was in fact an immense movement of population across the vacant spaces of the Eurasian steppe. In its European movement it overturned many established societies and contributed to the destruction of civilisation in Europe. But comparatively only a small section of this people reached the frontiers of India and though their pressure was continuous for over two centuries, they were finally defeated and driven out. Skanda Gupta who first withstood the onslaught of the barbarian hordes deserves a greater reputation in Indian history than has been accorded to him for it was he who destroyed the vigour of the first attack and blunted the spearhead. When a hundred years later the Huns again entered the Punjab and laid it waste under Toramana and Mihiragula, the momentum of their great movement had died. The Hun invasion had become a mere incident.

The victory of Skanda Gupta over the Huns which he celebrated in the Bhitari inscription may in its results be compared to the failure of the Huns earlier to subdue the Chinese Empire. "After three hundred years of fighting" says McGovern in his *Early Empires of Central Asia,* "the Huns and their Turanian allies were driven off into the West, with the eventual result that the Huns and their successors were destined to destroy not the Chinese but the Roman Empire."

The great Turki Empire in the 6th century, which ruled over an area extending from the Great Wall of China to Iran did not penetrate into India. But their occupation of Afghanistan was of some consequence to Indian defence.

Under two leaders of genius, Mukan and Tapo, the Turki tribes consolidated their rule and as other central Asian tribes before them entered the Afghan Valley in A.D. 640 forcing the Hindu Kush passes. The great Hindu Kingdom of Gandhara which was an advance post of India was destroyed by them. The Turki (Buddhist) rule collapsed temporarily and was succeeded by the Shahi (Hindu) Kingdom of Kabul which in turn was displaced by the Brahmin Kings of Ohind. When next the Turkis, now turned Muslim, entered the Afghan stage the Hindu monarchies of the area had become weak and disunited.

After the Huns the next serious invasion, potentially the most dangerous from every point of view, was that of Mahommed Bin Kassim on Sindh under the orders of the Khalif of Baghdad in A.D. 712. This was the great period of Arab expansion when from the borders of India to the borders of France the Arabs had overturned kingdoms, established dynasties and conquered and governed the most powerful empire of the time. This invasion by the greatest organised military power of the time has not received sufficient attention from historians. The general view, sedulously promulgated by Muslim chroniclers and following them the European historians, is that the Arab invasion of India through Sindh fizzled out for lack of support from Baghdad and the failure of initiative in Sindh. But what are the facts? After the battle of Raos in 712 when Ibn Kassim defeated Dehir, the Hindu King of Sindh, the whole of the lower Indus Valley from Multan to the sea fell under the Arabs. With their base firmly established on the Indian soil, they attempted to penetrate into Rajasthan from the land side and from the sea side to occupy Gujarat, Kutch, Saurashtra and Broach. If Junyad's expeditions had been successful Western India would have become a part of the Arab Empire, but the Chalukya Rulers and the Pratihara Emperors of Gujarat and Rajasthan were able in continuous fight, to destroy Arab power and to contain its remnants to the Sindh deserts.

Leaving aside Mahmud Ghazni's plundering raids, the conquest of the Gangetic Valley following the invasion of Mohammed Ghori, by Kutubuddin starts a new chapter in Indian history. But the general idea that these were Islamic invasions, part of the great upsurge of Islam to conquer the world for the faith, is historically untrue. With the decline of the Khalifs of Baghdad the expanding force of Islam from the religious point of view, ceased. The Khiljis, the Tughlaks and the Lodis who conquered North India and established their rule in the Gangetic Valley were Central Asian Turks, who in the historic process of their movement had become Muslims, very much in the same way as the Yue-chis or the Kushans, in their movement across the same area, had become Buddhists. The affiliations of the Delhi Sultans were not towards Arabia, or to the West but to Central Asia. In fact after the first generation, they settled down in India as exclusively Indian rulers with no interest outside.

The fact that they were Muslims had however one outstanding significance. While their predecessors from Turkistan, whether Kushans, Sakas or Huns were assimilated into Indian society and accepted Hindu culture, the new people from Turkistan because of their exclusive religion and the rigidity of their beliefs maintained their communal separateness. It was impossible to assimilate them, as time could not eliminate the differences, as in the case of the earlier peoples.

It is however interesting to note and necessary to emphasise that the geography of their dispersal followed the same pattern as the geography of Aryan dispersal. Their racial and cultural influence was greatest in the Punjab. By the time they settled in the Gangetic Valley, the dynamism of invasion was exhausted and the movement became almost exclusively political, the Sultans of Delhi, claiming to be Indian Rulers of Hindustan. They extended their authority to Bengal leaving the tablelands well alone as the Aryans had done before them. Another branch spread out to the South-West, holding Malwa and occupying Gujarat. But these were political developments and not population movements for, after a short interval we see the Rulers of Malwa and the Sultans of Gujarat allying themselves with Hindu Kings. Finally the power based on the Gangetic Valley, while able to carry out raids into the Deccan, was unable to conquer or hold peninsular India. The dispersal from the Gangetic Valley finds its term on the Vindhyas and the tide which had already lost its force breaks into billows against the mountain ranges of the Deccan.

The history of the Moghuls tells the same tale. This small backwash of the great population movement of the Mongols finally reaches India not as a world-shaking event as the conquests of Genghiz and his immediate successors were, but as a military adventure. But its geography is the same: from Ferganah to Kabul, from Kabul to Agra and with Agra the Gangetic Valley. Under Akbar the Empire is consolidated; Bengal is firmly held: a lightning campaign annexes Gujarat. The old areas of dispersal are in Moghul hands. Then begins the struggle. The armies of North India, with all the latest equipment available to a great power, open their campaigns against the Deccan. For over a hundred and ten years the might of the Moghul Empire is pitted against the geography of India and when Aurangzazib dies and the Empire is practically ruined the Moghuls had not penetrated beyond Tungabhadra. Within twenty-five years, the Marathas are on the move towards Malwa. The greatest and most deliberately organised campaign to bring the Deccan under the control of Delhi fails after an expenditure of men, treasure and effort to which Indian history shows no parallel.

Why is it that these great foreign invasions from the Aryans to the Moghuls spent themselves in the Gangetic Valley and were unable to touch the heart of India in the Deccan? This is the major secret of Indian history. The great population movements which overran Europe as in the case of the Aryans and the Huns, destroyed and laid waste everything up to the Carpathians as in the case of the Mongols, established new homelands in Western Asia and held half Europe under fee for 300 years as in the case of the Turks, exhausted themselves in the Punjab, spread out as a backwash in the Gangetic Valley, but failed to have any influence on the Deccan tablelands or on the South. The reason is to be found in the basic geographical factors. As Spykman, the noted American geographer, points out: "From Central Asia came the early invasions into the border zone, the eruptions of nomadic barbarians into Europe, Persia, India and China. Most persistent has been the pressure on Europe and China because *geography forces the flow of power into the East-West channel.* To the north lie Tundra waste and the polar sea. To the south stretches a zone of barren desert and the highest mountain barrier in the world (the Himalayas), in between an easy grass-land belt provides an area of mobility. Along this broad way the ancient horsemen of the plains exerted pressure on Vienna and Peking." This barbarian horde can find an outlet only across the Khyber Pass into the valley of the Indus and even to reach the pass they have to leave the broad highway, cross the Hindu Kush and establish themselves in the valleys of Afghanistan, by which time, deprived of the continuous flow of population, the movement loses a great deal of its momentum. India gets only a thin stream, whether it be of Aryans, of Huns, the Turks and the Mongols, for the main stream passes along the broad grass-lands.

The Hindu Kush is the outer area for the defence of the Indian sub-continent. But it is not an impassable range. There are three high-altitude passes from Central Asia into the Kunduz and Shorbard Valleys of Afghanistan which invaders, throughout history, used to cross into Afghanistan. The Indus Valley comes under threat once a military power is established in this area for there are routes from the Kabul Valley into the Punjab which have been known from the beginning of history. The two most famous are of course the Khyber Pass and the Passes into the lower Swat Valley. The British have given a mystic significance to the Khyber Pass, possibly because of their own experiences in the unfortunate Afghan campaigns. But Khyber was not the route favoured by the invaders of the past. Baber for example moved up the Kumar and debouched into the Lower Swat Valley. Alexander also seems to have preferred this line of advance.

It will be seen that the Afghan quadrilateral which looks a massive defence fortress became more or less a half-way house for invaders. The Aryans, the Kushans, the Huns, the Turks and the Moghuls used it in turn for this purpose. An anonymous geographer writing in the 10th century whose work has been edited by Prof. Minorsky states that Afghan area had four approaches. The same geographer affirmed that the gates of India were Bust, a site on the junction of the rivers Helmand and Arghandeb, a little to the west of Kandahar.

The other route into the Indian sub-continent, the Bolan Pass, though it seemed to have been used only once in history, by the Sakas, is not without importance. From Seistan it is not difficult to approach. The reason why in the past this route was neglected was perhaps entry through it led an invading force into the deserts of Sindh and Rajasthan. The Sakas who under pressure from the Yue-chi entered India via the Bolan Pass, were unable to establish a firm foothold in India.

What has preserved Indian civilisation in the past and saved it from being uprooted as the civilisations of the Nile and Tigris Valleys were, was her geographical position which lay out of the way of the main routes, protected by mountain barriers which only permitted a trickle of the great population currents to reach her; once having reached the densely populated Gangetic Valley, these invaders without constant reinforcements from their homelands, got submerged in the local population and further, even when their momentum carried them forward, the Deccan massif operated as a barrier strong enough to prevent their penetration to the South. Thus even when the Gangetic Valley fell under the domination of foreign culture as it often did during the last 2,000 years, Hindu civilisation was firmly entrenched in the South to maintain the continuity and provide the inspiration for a general revival.

So far we have dealt with invasions across the land frontier. The invasion by the sea nomads to which India was subjected during the last 450 years of her history presents different features. In 1498 Vasco da Gama's armed fleet arrived in the Indian seas round the Cape of

Good Hope and sailing across to Calicut from the African coast. Within a short period of 15 years his successors were able to establish a maritime empire which exercised steady and continuous pressure on the economy of India for centuries afterwards. The Portuguese closed all the sea routes to India and exercised a monopoly of Indian trade by the simple system of building bases round the Indian coast from where they patrolled the Indian seas and drove out all others who claimed the right to sail or trade. With naval stations in Malacca, Ceylon, Ormuz, and the African coast, and with a land base in Goa they exercised effective sovereignty over the Indian seas. But the Indian States of the time were too well organised and too powerful for the Portuguese to extend their influence on the land.

But pressure from the sea has a relentlessness which the sporadic threats from the side of the land do not possess. Once the coasts of a country become open to pressure from the sea, they remain perpetually under threat, for though the particular power which exercised the pressure might itself be destroyed, the indivisibility of the sea enables any other power, however distant, to step into the vacant place. Thus it was that England which had eliminated her rivals and established the mastery of the seas, stepped into the seats of power which Albuquerque had erected. From the middle of the 18th century, Britain was able to exercise continuous pressure on India's coast line. She was able to build up bases of power at Surat, Bombay, Madras and Calcutta when the land-based power of the Moghuls broke down at the centre and as a result of the new maritime economy, financial power shifted to the coast, sea power was able to undertake a systematic conquest of India such as no land power had ever done.

The routes of this invasion were also very different. Their power being based on the sea, the English first expanded into the two great river valleys, the two focii of Indian civilisation, the Cauvery Valley in the South and the Gangetic Valley in the North. From Madras they extended their authority first in the Tamil areas, and along the deltaic portions of the Andhra Coast. From Calcutta, they moved up slowly bringing under control the Indo-Gangetic Valley without any major military campaign. In a great pincer movement from the South across the Mysore tablelands and from Bengal across Central India, the land-based power of the Marathas was crushed in a campaign which culminated in Assaye. Slowly, for the first time, the whole of India passed under foreign rule. The relentless pressure of the sea, capable of bringing continuous reinforcements over thousands of miles, and moving steadily forward from its bases on the coast brought within a period of one hundred years the entire territory of India under occupation.

There are certain aspects of this conquest which require to be emphasised. In the first place, the most notable fact is that during the entire period of conquest and occupation (from A.D. 1757 to 1947) the invader remained a foreign power, the source of his authority and power remaining in a far off land. This is very different from the position of land powers, who whether Khiljis, Tughlaks or Moghuls became Indians in the first generation with the sources of their authority and power exclusively in India.

Secondly, the reinforcements from Europe were continuous and unending. From the time of the first fleet of Vasco da Gama there was an uninterrupted flow of power from the European ports to India, which continued even during the period of British occupation. As we noticed the position was totally different in the case of land powers which by this very fact were forced to become national.

Thirdly, all parts of India were equally under foreign rule though the form varied in the case of territories which were under the suzerainty of the Crown. While the bases of British strength continued to be the sea ports and the coastal areas, the weight of Britain's military strength was concentrated in the Punjab and the North-West Frontier so that both continental and Peninsular India were equally under control. The land powers based as they were on Delhi and the Gangetic Valley were never able to do this, with the result that except when the Centre was exceptionally strong under an able ruler, the periphery was but weakly held. The British had in fact no periphery, as the coastal and the Deccan areas which are the normal periphery of a land power, constituted their bases and their military strength was concentrated on the North-West Frontier.

Fourthly, their administration also continued to be mainly foreign with the superior personnel recruited from abroad and maintained, at least after the great Rebellion of 1857, in a constant state of preparedness.

Finally, with the government directed from a distant land and carried on by a predominantly foreign administrative machinery which had its origin in trade and economic exploitation, India became a colony, that is a territory governed in the interests of the metropolitan power. Her economic life, her trade and commerce, and the exportation of her natural resources were controlled by the conquering power. Invasions from land never had these results and could not in the nature of things lead to such developments.

In short, the British conquest of India, was the first real foreign conquest of the country. It was the first time in India's long history that she was ruled from outside her own territory. Small portions of India in the North-West had in the past been sometimes ruled as portions of a large empire. The Indus Valley was thus a part of the Empire of Persia. Portions of the Punjab had been annexed by the Rulers of Kabul at different times, for example, in the time of Ahmed Shah Durrani and Zaman Shah. But neither the Gangetic Valley nor the rest of India had ever been ruled from an outside capital by monarchs whose interests were external to India. Only the sea power was able to do this, for the indivisibility of sea enables any power which can establish undisputed mastery of the oceans to exert her power anywhere in the world and by long distance control rule over areas where land armies cannot easily reach.

The short-lived Japanese invasion of the Indian waters came from the eastern route, through the Straits of Malacca. Japan is situated in the Pacific many thousand miles away, but once the control of the sea passed to her through the conquest of Singapore, Indian Ocean lay at her mercy. That control which enabled her to send her ships to the Bay of Bengal was challenged not in the Indian Ocean but in far off Guadalcanal and the possibility of a landing in South India was thus averted. Japan's control of the sea was only a limited one, but in view of India's geographical position it was sufficient to enable her to land troops anywhere and create a base, if her power had not been challenged elsewhere.

We may briefly consider in this connection how air power has modified the situation as we have analysed it: the practical invulnerability of the Indian sub-continent from the land side, and its dangerous vulnerability from the side of the sea. To an invader from across the land frontier a superior air force will give additional strength, ground support, destruction of communications in the interior, dislocation of economic life through bombing, etc. But a conquest of India would be possible only through sustained military effort across long distances through difficult passes and under trying climatic conditions. The Himalayas with their dreary uplands, the Hindu Kush and its ranges will still remain major problems. If India has also an effective air force capable of continued defensive operations, the danger from the land side is greatly minimised as the routes of invasion are limited and can be effectively defended. The position is altogether different in the case of pressure from the side of the sea. With adequate air cover, an invading force could select its own place of landing, can be continuously reinforced and hold and enlarge its base. The physical features of the Indian Ocean do not, as we have seen, give island cover to the coast to enable serious interception operations at sea. Even if it did, the American campaign in the Pacific from the Guadalcanal to the very shores of Japan, to Okhinawa, would demonstrate that overwhelming sea power has an island or a peninsula at its mercy, if not for conquest at least for effective attack. The coastal waters of every country belong in effect to the state that has control of the seas, which involves also air power.

CHAPTER VI

CONCLUSION

GEOPOLITICS we have defined as the study of the state in space, that is an attempt to analyse and understand the permanent political factors arising from the geographical features of a country. That geographical features are more permanent and therefore their influences more abiding need hardly be emphasised. The Himalayas are an unchanging factor in Indian history; so is the Indian Ocean. We can but study their influence, take account of them and turn them to our advantage. The other physical factors may to a large extent be remediable; for example irrigation may change the arid character of a country; science may remedy the deficiencies of the soil; new inventions may find substitutes for the natural resources that a country lacks. But in order to do all this, it is necessary that we should know clearly the geographical factors that affect our national life. This is what I have sought to do in a preliminary way in this essay. I propose in this chapter to summarise and sort out my conclusions and to see whether any lessons can be learnt from our discussion of geographical factors in Indian history.

The first conclusion I would draw is that geography has enforced on us two Indias, one which may be described Aryavarta, with its centre in the Gangetic Valley and the other the Deccan, extending from the Vindhyan region to the tip of the Peninsula. Racially, linguistically and politically these have remained separate. Their unity has been through culture, religion and a classical language, Sanskrit, which, though foreign in origin, became pre-eminently a national language shaping the mind of the people from the Himalayas to Cape Comorin and moulding their thought and speech in a way which no other language has done.

These two Indias have now been united politically and this was brought about by the fact that a sea power enveloping India had conquered the whole country and forcibly united it as no land power had been able to do in the past. Britain was enabled to do this by the fact that the attack being from the sea it had no one base as a land based invasion would have had to, but two bases to begin with and later on three from which they were able to cover her entire area. The two focii of Indian civilisation, the Gangetic Valley and the Cauvery Plains were the areas first conquered, and for a power based on the sea, it was not difficult to fan out from these bases.

Since the political and administrative unity of India has now been achieved in spite of difficulties which had been found insurmountable in the past, it is our primary duty not to lose it again and to overcome through our effort such obstacles as stand in the way of complete unification. But the lessons of both geography and history are clear here. Any attempt to impose a unification by the more populous North over the people of the South will be disastrous, for it will awaken the latent racial feelings of difference and geography will again tend to assert itself. The bonds of political unity which have been brought into existence must be strengthened by economic integration between the two areas, by giving to the Deccan its legitimate influence in political affairs, by maintaining steady contact between the two regions, by encouraging the development of southern culture in the north, etc. All policies which look like an

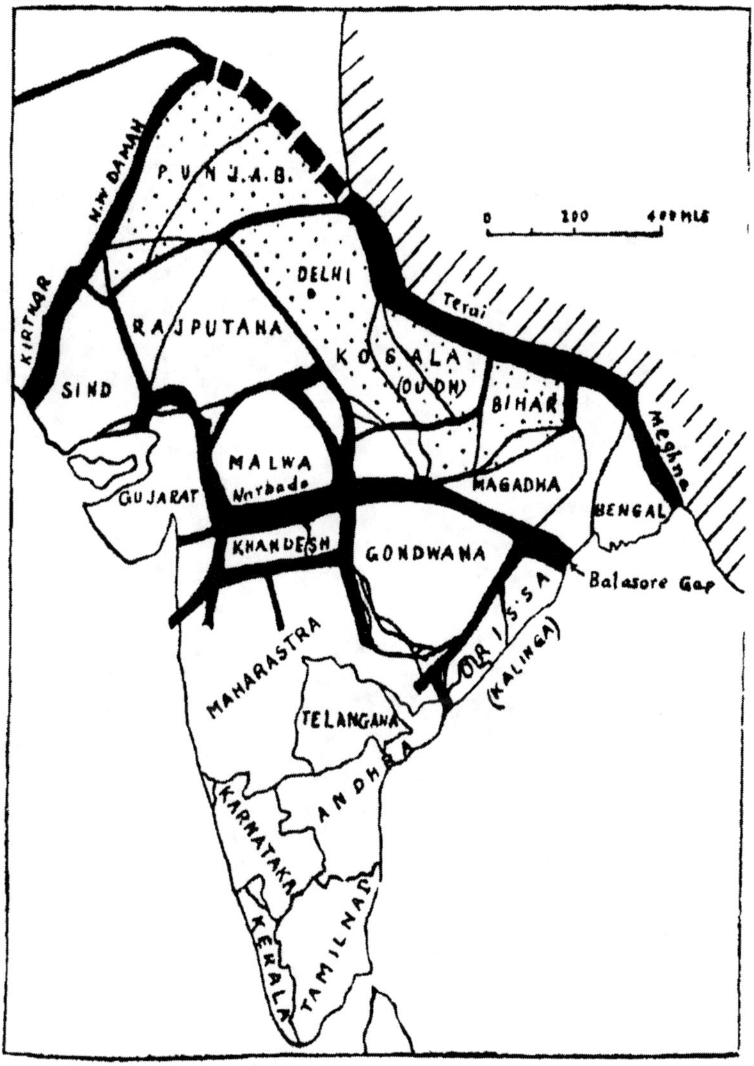

India—Basic Historic Divisions

imposition of northern authority over the South should be avoided.

A truly national army recruited without reference to areas, regions and classes can be a great instrument to secure cohesion. In all multi-lingual countries armed forces have always been a precious crucible for the transmutation of provincialism into an integral nationalism. No past empire in India had this advantage. The northern empires which attempted to conquer the South tried to do so with northern soldiers. The Maharattas who attempted to conquer the North did so with a Deccani army. Even the Sepoy Army of the British became after the conquest of the Punjab mainly a North Indian force, based on an artificial division between martial and non-martial classes. For the first time in our history we have a truly national army, air and naval forces recruited without reference to areas, classes or castes, but representing broadly every part of India.

Closer economic integration, making the areas mutually dependent is also important. So far there has been no such planning. Though our five-year plan takes all-India factors into consideration, the necessity of bringing about a greater union between geographically different areas is not there. The economics of the north and the south have remained different.

An equally important point which should not be forgotten is the development of road and rail communications between the north and the south. There is a general impression that now since air communication with every part of India is easy, road and rail services have lost much of their importance. This is a dangerously erroneous point of view. Air communication only hops from place to place and does not have the advantages of either opening up areas in between, or of bringing about intercourse between peoples. On the other hand, where roads and railways penetrate the areas are opened up and greater contacts between peoples are established. We have already noticed that one of the main weaknesses of India is that there are no natural lines of communication between the north and the south. From the time that Agastya traversed the Vindhya range and went to the South, such routes as were opened up have been used only by pilgrims, and occasional conquerors and not for any considerable population movements or for large-scale trade. The absence of rivers flowing from the North to the South or *vice versa* owing to the geographical structure of the country has also contributed greatly to this weakness. British policy in the matter of rail and road communications emphasised the north-south differences. Their main railway lines were laid for purposes of maritime trade, to convey to the sea at Bombay and Calcutta the produce of the Gangetic Plain and strategically to connect the different ports. Their road system was also based mainly on strategic considerations relating to the North-West Frontier. It is not surprising therefore to find that direct railway connection between Delhi and the South was established by a circuitous route only almost at the end of British rule in India. A programme of national highways connecting the major areas of the South with northern India is an urgent necessity to remedy our geographical weakness.

I have alluded to the fact that the one major unifying factor in Indian history is the dominance of Sanskrit as the language of higher thought in India. I should like to quote what I have said in another connection about the exceptional importance of this great language in maintaining our unity:

"Earlier, I said that Sanskrit is the one common national inheritance of India. The South and the North, the West and the East have equally contributed to it. No part of India can claim it as its exclusive possession. When we talk of our national genius being unity in diversity, of the fundamental oneness of Indian mind, etc., what we are really meaning is the dominance of Sanskrit which overrides the regional differences and linguistic peculiarities and achieves a true national character in our thought and emotions and even gives form and shape to the languages. So far as I know there has never been an instance in world history when a language which was but the speech of an invading few was able to establish its unchallenged authority over a whole sub-continent and be its permanently unifying factor for over two thousand years. Sanskrit is India's one national language and whatever position Hindi may achieve as *vyavahara bhasha* or the common language of the future, the unity of India will collapse if it ceases to be related to Sanskrit or breaks away from the Sanskritic tradition. Sanskrit alone has that pre-eminence which Hindi could never claim, over the great regional languages, enabling her to maintain and uphold in every region of India the supreme claim of Indian unity. It may indeed be said that one who knows Sanskrit is a better Indian for he is in a position to appreciate what every part of India has contributed to it. With Vyasa he could roam about in the forests and pilgrimage centres of the whole country, with Valmiki he could visit Lanka, with Kalidas see the glories of Ujjain, walk in the Himalayan valleys, or follow the cloud from Ramagiri to Kailas, with Bhartrihari contemplate on the vanities of the world, with the merchants of Somadeva travel to *dwipantaras* and even to Kanakapuri, with Sudraka live the life of a gay *nāgarika*. Through Sanskrit we get something added to us from every part of India. Kalhana makes us live with the kings of Kashmir. With Jona Raja we share in the glory of Prithviraja. We take from Jayadeva some of his ecstasy, from Hemachandra Suri his gift of being able to illumine almost anything. With Queen Gangadevi of Vijayanagar we march on Madura. With Bhavabhuti we sport on the Godavari. With Dandin we are at the Pallava court at Kanchi. With Narayana Bhatta we are in Kerala. With Jagannatha Pandita we taste a little of the magnificence of Shah Jehan."

The point I should like to emphasise is that while it is not only desirable but necessary that Hindi, based primarily on Sanskrit, should become the common *vyavahara bhasha* of India, unless we take simultaneous steps to maintain and uphold the position of Sanskrit as a common language of higher thought—a position which does not conflict with the claims of Hindi as the common language, or the rights of our great regional languages—the cultural unity of India, which is our strongest bond, cannot be maintained for any length of time. Regional languages will become more and more independent with nothing to unite them to a common Indian mind, for Hindi will never fulfil that purpose, however prevalent it may become as the language of the State.

The over-riding and governing fact of all political thinking in every country is its own security, its survival as a nation. It is here that geographical considerations come to have a pre-eminent importance. It is to this aspect of the question that we should now turn. We have noticed that India is so situated that she could be attacked both from the land side and from the side of the sea. From the land side we are protected to a very large extent and the invasions which have taken place have at all times lost themselves in the plains of the Ganges. Apart from the military adventures of ambitious or avaricious rulers like Alexander, Mahmud of Ghazni, or Nadir Shah, the invasions of India from the land side have been the result of unsettled conditions in Central Asia leading to great movements of population, a section of which reaches the Kabul Valley and from there enters India. In historic times such movements have taken place once every three hundred years though their strength and intensity have varied according to the time lag which these movements take to reach the Indian frontier.

The basic fact about the invasions from Central Asia is that they are sporadic and dependent on unsettled conditions in that area. There has never been any continuous pressure on the land frontier of India by any foreign power. Owing to the geographical factors which we have discussed, whether, with the organisation of powerful states covering the vacant spaces of Central Asia, such a threat will now materialise, is a problem for military leaders and not for geographers. Whether it does or not, the factors of distance, space and other obstacles remain.

From the side of the sea the position is different. The fact that we have had numerous invasions from the land side and only one invasion from the sea side has made us believe that the danger from the land side is greater and more permanent and the danger from the sea is less important. That there has been only one invasion from the sea is due to the fact that the invasion route to India came to be discovered only in 1498. It is necessary to emphasise that from that historic day when Vasco da Gama with his fleet of warships arrived at Calicut, India has ever been under the relentless pressure of sea power, steady and unseen over long periods, but effectively controlling our economic life and political life. In fact since 1498, India has been blockaded, and British authority in India was based on the iron ring fence of the Royal Navy which controlled the Indian Ocean. Therefore while the threat from the land side is sporadic and is effective only under given conditions, the threat from the sea is ever present and perpetually effective. We have been misled by our history into neglecting this aspect by comparing the number of sporadic raids and invasions from across the land frontier to the number of invasions from the sea, forgetting that once the route was opened up India's economy lay at the mercy of marauding sea nomads and her political independence was always under continual pressure from organised sea power.

In respect of sea power, there is no such thing as a vacuum. The indivisibility of the sea makes it subject to the strength of nations situated far away. Even if therefore, it is assumed, I believe erroneously, that British naval power has ceased to be effective in the Indian Ocean, others even more powerful are ready to fill such a hypothetical vacuum. In fact Britain, with bases in Singapore, Trincomalee and Aden still controls the Indian Ocean as effectively as she did when she had the control of India. Nor would her withdrawal from the Indian Ocean help us as it would only mean the ocean passing under the control of other naval powers who may be less scrupulous in the exercise of their power. The blockade of the China Coast on flimsy pretexts should open our eyes to what a naval power can do even in times of peace.

There is however one saving factor in regard to sea power. It is wholly ineffective against organised land masses. Even in India, sea power, though dominant on even the coastal waters of the country and exercising an absolute monopoly of India's trade and shaping her commercial economy to European needs, was at the mercy of the Moghul Emperors on land, so long as a strong central government existed in India. Similar was the case with China. European history also teaches the same lesson. So long as the land power is strong and effective the nomads of the sea can only raid and destroy coastal areas and control the trade. But once the central power decays and weakens, the sea powers are able to occupy coastal areas and exercise political authority. After a hundred years of effort England had to give up her policy of territorial conquest in France. The experience of France in Mexico, of Japan in China, all tell the same tale. Once the land mass is organised, the danger of invasion from the sea is not great, though the pressure of sea power, as we have said, will be always there and always ready to utilise any opportunities arising from the weaknesses of the land based state. The only practical remedy to this permanent geographical weakness of India, its exposed position in regard to powers operating from the sea, is the strength of her own internal political and economic structure. Of course the best and most effective reply is to develop our own naval power, strong enough to exercise control over the waters necessary for our defence. That does not seem an immediately practical proposition, though there is nothing to prevent us doing so, considering that Japan with much less resources was able to develop her naval strength within a period of 30 years. But even the development of naval strength postulates a strong central government having full control of the resources of the nation, a very high level of industrialisation, a political and economic integration of the country, which would overcome the internal contradictions present in our society, an advancement in scientific research and technical application of such research as would raise us to the level of a powerful state. The growth of our naval power itself would be dependent on these and if we reach that stage of development, there is no question of our independence being threatened by any power though the sea may continue to be menacing.

Continuous vigilence is the price of freedom, but the vigilence we exercise must be based on an understanding of the elements of our strength and weakness, the potentialities of those who are matched against us, of the rise and decay of centres of power in areas of interest to us, etc. In the past we were utterly ignorant of political developments outside the Indian border and never realised the danger till it was at our door-step. We had absolutely no knowledge of the sources of European power long after Vasco da Gama reached the Indian shores. In fact Europe came into our vision only in the 19th century. The importance of sea power was never recognised by the great North Indian Empires, and in the South the idea of oceanic control was absent as the sea was considered a free element and only the protection of the coast was considered the duty of the state. It is therefore ignorance that was responsible for India's political downfall, ignorance combined with a lack of appreciation of geographical factors within India itself. India had neither a continental view like China or Persia, or an oceanic view like Japan. Ensconced between the mountain ranges and enveloped by the sea, she looked upon all outsiders who occasionally intruded into her country as *mlechas* who had to be driven out if possible, or tolerated if they could not be driven out, and as the *mlechas* never came in too great a force India was able to survive.

Today what we require is both a continental view and an appreciation of sea power. No longer can we be satisfied with the geography of the Jambudwipa when the world has contracted and power groupings even in the most distant parts of the globe affect our life. Geopolitics has therefore to become an essential subject of study for all interested in the future of India, for as we have seen, we could only neglect it at our peril.

INDEX

F

G

H

I

J

R

S